THE DASH
between the dates
on their tombstone.

Betty Barkman

PRESS

The Missing Link

———o/o/o———

$\mathcal{E}$veryone has at least a few regrets. It's par for our course - as humans.

One of my most haunting ones, and most complicated, too, involves a missing link in my repertoire of how I honoured my father and mother.

As a child, I, of course, considered my parents pretty perfect. Most children do. But again as happens so often, that changed drastically during my teens. Granted, I was looking through tinted glasses clouded by various forms of rebellion on my part. I had no intention of being wayward, ever, but I was always tugging at the bit. Nevertheless, regardless of whose fault it was, this is what I saw. A father who was super-strict, super-conservative, unyielding and frequently harsh, saying no to almost everything I asked for. A mother who was unable to give me what I craved for most – understanding. And support toward my spiritual journey which I needed so badly, but she had enough issues of her own to bog her down, it seemed, and these were very real. Their marital relationship seemed to have reached an all time low as well. Just watching them struggle drove me to despair – making me flee to the outhouse for respite time and again. . .

I also became a Christian as a teenager. I loved God and wanted nothing more than to serve Him. As I learned about the necessity of forgiving, I decided, quite innocently, to do just that regarding all my hurts. I thought that meant sweeping things under the rug and pretending they didn't matter. For some people, that may work. For me, it was, without knowing it myself, like putting a pot to simmer on the backburner and hoping nobody, neither myself or others, would notice.

Life went on. I married young. My husband and I had a good relationship with my parents. We visited regularly and helped each other out as needs would arise. I'll never forget the day when I was unexpectedly sick in bed, and our oldest daughter, who must have been about six, secretly called my parents for help. Within an hour, they were there - ready to do whatever was needed. And that was only one of the times.

Shortly before Christmas in 1970, when mother was diagnosed with cancer, it was a double whammy. Father had just been diagnosed with Alzheimer's. When her cancer came back with renewed vengeance after what had been thought to be a successful surgery, we as a family decided to care for her at home so that we could provide for both parents at the same time. And that's what we did, taking turns. It wasn't easy. All of us had housefuls of young children who, at first, came along to *help*, but as the situation grew worse, had to be *farmed* out to others who were willing to stand in the gap. Yet we did it out of love, genuine Godly love, no strings attached.

On September 16 in '71, Mother succumbed to the cancer. I was 32. Our 1 year old daughter had learned to walk at her deathbed.

Father came to our homes to be cared for now. Although we had applied at Bethesda Personal Care Home, there was a waiting list, and we hated the thought of bringing him there anyway; it was against his will. So, we did what we had to do. At our house, he spent a total of seven months – seven very challenging and yet very rewarding months. The Lord filled our hearts with love and joy in spite of the difficulties, and even our children have fond memories of that season. When the call came from Bethesda, it saddened me. I could have kept him longer, but we held a family consensus, and then brought him in. Two months later, he was gone – succumbed to pneumonia.

I was parentless, and I grieved my loss, but I had done my part to honour and respect and care for them in their time of need, hadn't I? So why would I now struggle with regrets?

In 1975, I started figuring it out, but never quite finished dealing with it or taking that final step. The finding and the telling of this story is *that* step - the missing link.

That year, God knocked me over the head, so to speak, with a 2' by 4' when I was at the Health Science Center for the 11 week-long, life-and-death-style delivery of our youngest son. I realized then to my dismay that I had, like the third character in the Bible story about talents, been burying things in the garden instead of giving them to God. My flair for simple writing like this was one of those *hidden-down-under* things. But I learned that I couldn't really unearth *that* without opening up the whole can of worms which included festering bits of bitterness. The old hurts had not really ever left – I had been blind to that, and now God was opening my eyes.

How I wish someone somewhere would have taught me about true forgiveness. And overcoming the pain. Or that I could teach someone else about that now. It is *so* important!

But eventually, I learned. And grew. The sweating palms and stand-up hair began to happen less and less often, even when I recalled the unhappy events and gradually, I've had a harder time listing the pains. It's as if they have dissipated, and I praise God for that. He is good!

Back to my regrets though. Where does all this fit in with honouring my parents? I warned you in the beginning that this might seem complicated, but I'll try to say it in plain English.

My regrets are that, due to my ignorance and blindness and youthful rebellion of one kind or another, I never got to really know my parents. By the time I realized that, it was too late. Yes, I had loved them passionately, thankfully blood is thicker than water, so that wasn't the problem. In my youth, I had seen what I saw, and there's no denying that. What I missed out on was seeing life from *their* perspective, figuring out what made them tick, *why* they were what they were, the *reason* behind things. I had never asked them questions about their own childhood. Especially, and this is a biggie, I had never zoned in on and admired and appreciated their long list of amazing and strong qualities.

Of this, I have repented, and I've asked God to send an angel to share that with my parents. And I have changed. With great pleasure, I could now tell you all about the good things - something I used to be unable to do.

But there was this aspect that was yet undone. I had still never researched their stories.

And I'd had a growing conviction that this is what I needed to do. I am, after all, a story teller, I believe by God's design.

So, finally, I have done it and here we are. This is their story, based on both my many hours of research and my now genuinely aroused imagination. The kind of facts that can be verified are – no apologies there, and every scene has its full share of those. Then truth starts trickling down to diaries and memoires, to my own fragmented memories of comments that took me sometimes years to figure out, or to overheard conversations dating back more than fifty years, and to the many memories by relatives as they've been so generously shared with me. Finally, to fill in the gaps, especially of their earlier years where my helpers were hardest to find, I have used my imagination, sticking as close to the known truth as I found humanly possible considering that pictures and recordings are not available and that I have not yet discovered a better way of telling an old story as it really happened.

Is the story true? Definitely. But it is also creatively written, and I will leave it to every reader to figure out how the two blend. Or, you can just enjoy the read without being quite sure which is which. You might have a hard time re-verifying things if you tried. In the end, does it really matter?

I pray you will be blessed as you read, that my parents (from their long time heavenly vantage point) will be honoured, and that God's name will be glorified. He is good!

Sincerely,

Their oldest daughter,
Betty

P.S. You will want to read the epilogue, too.

TINA'S

STORY

Tina Kornelsen Wiebe December 23, 1907 – September 16, 1971

—❦—

Preface - 1918

—⊂◦⫟◦⊃—

$\mathscr{I}$ had always liked school, but this had to be one of its best hours yet. I absolutely loved the song Teacher had just taught us.

It was lively and interesting.
It was modern.
It had a fun beat.
And it was English. Mr. Reimer certainly had not found this one in the church's old black *Gesangbuch*. I was convinced it was at least a little naughty, too.

Very carefully, I copied every line into my thin, shiny black scribbler which I kept for just such days, making sure I didn't miss a word.

Keep on the sunny side, always on the sunny side
Keep on the sunny side of life . . .
It will help you every day
It will guard you all the way
If you'll only
Keep on the sunny side of life . . .
It will lighten all your way
It will turn your night to day
If you'll only
Keep on the sunny side of life . . .

"Teacher," I called out before I could remind myself to obey the rules. He looked my way and was ready for my question, regardless.

"How can a person keep on the sunny side of life?'

He looked surprised, but still he answered, "That's a good question." And he seemed to be reflecting some before he continued with genuine warmth in his tone. "I think it takes two things. One is trusting God. People who trust God have much more chance of seeing the sunshine in life. But the second thing is probably just as important, maybe even more so. That is, we need to stop griping about all the bad things that happen to us and instead count and appreciate and dwell on the blessings that God has already given us."

Really?

For me, that was a mouthful. It gave me food for many thoughts.

One day, my best friend, Anna, was not at school, and I wasn't in the mood for being with anyone else at recess time. I sauntered back into the classroom and sat down at my spot at one of the long desks in the now empty room. Finally, I'd have a chance to figure this out.

It seemed natural for me to think about the bad things that kept happening to me. The list was long and growing. I needed all my fingers to make even a quick rundown.

The bull run was only the first that came to mind. My brother Gerhard and I had been getting the cows home together that day. I could still taste the fear and the sweat as we made our great escape underneath the loose section of the page wire fence.

And, of course, the big black bear adventure, in the north pasture, all by my lonesome.

Or the lightning hitting us smack in the middle of our little house and scaring us all half to death.

All the irritations were part of it, too. Guys at school pulling my braids, brothers bugging me endlessly, never having space or anything else to call my own, Pa giving me goose bumps of fear when he was upset, Ma crying when she thought no one was looking, all of us needing to work so hard all the time with hardly ever a retrieve or reward.

Should I simply have chalked all that off as being part of a family that has thirteen children, including my nine brothers, and being dirt poor at that?

Perhaps. Some things were bigger though. Like the stuff that had been happening in the barn when Ma and Pa weren't home. I'd been told in no uncertain terms that decent folks did not talk about such things. Not now. Not ever. Did that make it wrong for me to even think about it on my own?

And the newest hurt now - this thing about my eye. I had so hoped that Pa would see the urgency and be able to help. But Mr.Reimer's fervent plea had made no difference. Pa's answer remained firm – the strongest "no" I'd ever heard from him yet. As far as I could see, there was not a hope in the world.

Teacher had said to stop griping and start counting the good things. How could I do that? Where did I start? I so much longed to somehow get to the sunny side of life like the song said. If he was right and that's what it took, I must learn. There had to be a way.

I could start with one thing. I love my Ma. She's a good woman - yet her life is tough. Would it count if I did something special for her, maybe a surprise of some kind? I'd have to think . . um . . .

Shucks! Recess is over already?

Tomorrow I would come up with more good things on my list. Surely I would; I must.

Chapter One

———◊◊◊———

Early summer, 1916

I ran; brambles and tree branches scratched and slapped me like hands reaching out, trying to grab me. I ran pell-mell, beating at the limbs, looking for the trail, falling over rotting logs, getting up again and darting first to the left, then to the right. A fallen limb caught my ankle, and down I went again, harder this time. How could that trail have disappeared so entirely?

I had to make it out of these woods. Right now, not later.

Sobbing, I prayed, "Help me, God. Help me. Let me get away," as I groped my way along, stooped under branches, clambered over even more half rotten logs, and pushed my way through tangled thickets. The evening sun cast long shadows, moving about eerily to frighten me even more.

Never, never would I have volunteered to enter the north woods by myself. This is where all the wild things were. But I'd had no choice. When Pa says go, you go. And when Pa says bring, you bring. Except this time, I didn't. I couldn't. I had thought I'd be okay. Indeed, everything had been quite fine until I stumbled upon Molly, the big black cow, dozing all by herself.

I'd found a fresh, long stick like we usually used for chasing cows. Sticks always helped; we children felt braver, tougher somehow; the cows more compliant. I was muttering her name, pointing the stick, ready to swing it down hard, very close to pouncing upon her, when suddenly she lifted her head and I saw . . .

Ach, I couldn't believe it. A bear? How could I have been so fooled?

At first, my legs wouldn't move. *What's wrong with them?* And then as I saw the creature slowly rise, my adrenalin kicked in; I turned and ran. Now I couldn't get away fast enough.

When I came to the stream that meandered through both meadows, I knew where I was. I swiped at the tears that blurred my vision and looked hurriedly for the dead elm tree trunk that Pa and my brothers had slung across it as a bridge. The ground was a little smoother here, and though still shaded by towering trees, it looked worn and traveled. Perhaps this was where elk and deer came to drink and coyotes prowled at night. I shivered.

At last, I found it. Gingerly, I crossed it, too, crying out as I wobbled and flailed my arms for balance. I did not fall. For one split second, I was glad I was alone – at least there were no smirking brothers to contend with. Then, when I heard once more the heavy crashing noise somewhere behind me, I shook in terror. Gasping and whimpering, I struggled forward, and then suddenly, I found the trail, a narrow, hoof-trodden path of dirt winding through the tall trees and bushy shrubs. I followed it anxiously; careful not to get lost again, yet I hurried as fast as I dared over the still rough, uneven ground.

And then, I was in the open meadow. And I could see home.

Taking no chances, I rushed on, panting and gasping for breath, not letting myself stop until I tumbled in by the garden gate - good thing it was hanging half open - and threw myself on the ground. I tried to catch my breath; it felt like rambles of rasps and wheezes.

The house door slammed and Ma came running. "What's wrong, Child? What's wrong?"

I found no answer. Ma started shaking me, and finally, I blurted. "A bear. A bear. A big, black bear." I started to get up, but stumbled dizzily and fell back again.

Ma's voice sounded gruff when she took command. "Stay down, Tina, stay down. I will go and get Pa."

Pa was in the back yard, sharpening scythes. He wasn't usually good at handling interruptions, but when Ma told him what she knew, he immediately dropped his work and hollered for the boys to come and help. With one stout stick and two garden hoes in hand, they set out on their bear hunt. While I kept trying to recapture my normal breathing, Ma tended to my scrapes and bruises.

About an hour later, Pa and the boys were back, tired, droopy and empty handed, having found large footprints and the nesting site but nothing more. I was relieved. That monster of a bear would not have been a good match for the three of them without guns.

Darkness was descending rapidly now. All at once, everyone remembered the cows, still not at home. Who would go for them, now? And worse, where might they actually be? The day had been very hot and sultry, and that's when cows sometimes get ornery, with a mind of their own. They could be hiding – who knows where? Even Pa and the boys in their frenzy had forgotten about them until now.

Suddenly, our heads all jerked around as we heard a distinct and familiar mooing. It was close at hand, too. Peering intently into the almost-night like shadows, I could just make out the shapes. All nine head; five cows, two steers, and two little calves were coming home single file, marching directly up to the barn's back door.

"Well, what do you know?" Pa said. This time, there was no roughness in his voice, and he glanced around at his family with a kind and thankful look.

July 1917

The sweltering heat had continued non-stop for more than a week now. Even at night, there was little relief. When I climbed up the ladder to the bedroom space I shared with my 16-year-old sister Liz, everybody called her Liesche, and our brothers – our girl-part sectioned off by a quilt strung along on a wire, a wire that refused to stop sagging no matter how many times we tightened it - I nearly fell backward. The stifling, hot air slapped me in the face much like the oven heat did when I pulled out Ma's baking. But I had no choice. One thing was certain, when I spent much of the night panting and puffing and sweating profusely, even right beside the open window, I felt too groggy to get up in the morning. Never mind counting the moths that had been killed, or reckoning with the angry mosquitoes that buzzed around my ears, which, when they succeeded in their hunt for my blood, left swollen inch-wide welts that itched relentlessly for a whole long week.

Yet sometimes, like today, getting up in the morning offered some sort of relief.

The weather was going to change. The drumming, urgent-sounding noise of the mosquitoes was telling us. And Ma was telling us- she could feel it in her bones. And Pa was telling us, he could see it in the air, he said, and in the clouds. I didn't understand. How could anyone know such things?

My sister and I - some of our brothers were helping, too - had been picking peas early in the morning and were now spending long, boring hours shelling them. It was nobody's favorite job, but it had to be done. 6-year- old Gerhard brought in a handful of young carrots. Quickly, I grabbed one for myself and started munching on it. *Yummy good,* I thought as I started scrubbing the rest of them down, slicing them before adding them to one of the big bowls of ready-to-can peas. The jars, which the boys had brought up from the dingy little cellar, had already been washed. Ma and Liz were rapidly filling them and now started sealing them. The large, oval, battered copper boiler, half filled with water , was sitting on the warming end of the kitchen stove, waiting to do its thing as soon as enough jars would be ready and the fire built up hot enough to heat that monstrosity. Heinrich and Isaac had filled the wood box extra high.

Ma sighed as she worked. *If only we had a summer kitchen, so we could keep this mess and the HEAT of the canning outside.* I knew her thoughts well. She'd said it often enough. With a touch of fierce determination, Ma sounded more cheerful when she said, "Pa says perhaps next summer we will build that new house we've all been dreaming about. Then, this will be our extra space and summer kitchen." Liz grunted, "He's said that before." I hoped Ma hadn't heard her. It wasn't fair. *We all know it's only been five years since we moved to our own farm, and they haven't been easy years either. Give Pa a break.*

I didn't always feel that charitable toward Pa. There were days when my feelings about him were turbulent, bouncing up and down all over the place. But not today.

Suddenly the kitchen door burst open. *Pa is home. And he looks upset. What's going on?*

I didn't have time to wonder long. Pa's voice was even more brusque than usual. "Stop working right now," he fairly shouted. "Don't you see those awful clouds coming up?" He looked accusingly at Ma, then at the seven children scattered round about her, each trying somehow to *help* in her pea canning bee. Before anybody moved, there was a loud crashing thunderclap and little Bernhard screamed. Pa grabbed him, hushed him up, and immediately started manoeuvring everyone into the tiny sitting room that doubled as a master bedroom and held two children's beds besides, three if you counted the double for two.

I turned and stared out the west window. There was a blackness that looked eerie, almost as dark as night. *And this is early afternoon. Pa is right. Something terrible is happening.* Obediently, everyone huddled in a circle in the room. Only Pa was standing. Pacing. Restless. Watching the door. Suddenly, I understood. Two of my brothers were missing. They'd been helping him with the haying. Had they decided to stay in the barn after putting the horses in, or were they still on the field with the team?

I dared not ask.

For about half an hour perhaps – it felt like much more - lightning flashed, thunder raged, wind howled, and rain came down in torrents. We waited it out together, tightly, obediently, gasping in awareness at every piece of fresh and noisy evidence – *God is speaking.*

And then, just as fast as it came, it was over. And other than the generous sprinkling of twigs and branches all over the place – one tree, the twisted old maple was completely uprooted - and the humungous water puddles that my brothers suddenly felt a great need to explore, nothing much had happened. We were none the worse for it.

So, back to our pea canning bee we went.

August 15, 1917

Once again, a set of dark, threatening clouds was aligning itself in the west. This could be a bad storm, maybe even worse than last time. The sky was getting awfully dark – black and blue and purple all mixed together, I noticed. But there was no time to dwell on that.

How many storms can happen in one summer?

This time, everybody made it home; even at mid-afternoon and everybody, yes, everybody, rushed into the little house to find shelter. We huddled together, closely, quietly, just like Pa had taught us. *You always, always show respect for a thunderstorm, because that is God's voice speaking.* I couldn't tell you how often I had heard those words spoken. but the feeling of them was so deeply ingrained in my brain, it must have been many times. Ma was having goose bumps, I could tell. She never did like storms.

The thunder claps were getting louder and sharper, not just closer, but closer together, one right after the other. We huddled harder as the darkness became eerier.

At a particularly loud bang, Ma jumped and then clung to Pa. Five year old Berhard starting whimpering breathlessly, quite forgetting his own little code of ethics.

At the next blast, the whole house began to shake. Whimpers increased and gasps came from everyone now.

And then it happened. The unthinkable. The unwanted. The untrained for.

A brilliant light enveloped us, followed by a tiny split second of unreal silence before the whole world, in one gigantic crashing ambush, exploded. Or so it seemed. Every one of us fell backwards or sideways or whatever way, tumbling all over each other, and for a moment, just lay there, stunned, in shock, not moving.. Nobody said a word. Not even Pa.

Then slowly, groggily, Pa began picking himself up and looking around. That was all the cue we needed. We all started wiggling and gingerly trying to sit up. Soon, some of the boys were upright.

Every eye stared, every mouth gaped, every mind buzzed. *Are we dead or alive? What happened?*

Pa finally found his voice. "Is everybody okay?' He sounded croaky in the hush that enveloped us and felt almost sacred.

We gaped at ourselves and each other, but before any of us came up with an answer for Pa, we began to absorb the next factor- *the horrible mess that had somehow landed amongst us.* Where did that come from? Everything in the whole house as well as each one of us was covered with soot and ashes. Strange looking splinters were strewn around at crazy angles. Suddenly, we became aware of splattering noises and felt the rain coming down on our heads.

I followed Pa's gaze to the ceiling. There was a jagged, gaping hole right through the roof, right through our bedroom, the children's bedroom in the little loft. The lightening bolt had hit in or around the chimney and smashed its way right through the house. On the wooden floor, huge splinters were poking out in every direction. The stove pipes were down, helter-skelter like and bent out of shape from the impact. It was amazing that no one had been knocked out cold when they busted down on us, but the soot and ashes may well have come from there. Or perhaps from the wood stove whose cast-iron hole covers had lifted and were now sitting at precarious angles.

Good thing it rained. Otherwise, the house would surely have burned down. Now, it only smelled like it had. Or maybe worse.

The repercussions of that hit were horrendous. First, there was the physical clean up. Not only did everything and every-body have to get thoroughly scrubbed, and I mean *thoroughly* scrubbed with lye soap, and so much repair work had to be done, it took the joint efforts of the whole family a couple of long days to accomplish it.

Then, there were the more-or-less hidden aspects. Pa developed chest pains from that day on, and it was believed that, even the doctor said so, his heart had been damaged. He had already not been strong like he used to be even before this. But this incident became his turning point for the worse. Having a father who was energetic, ambitious, and strong quickly became only a distant memory.

For Ma, it was a nervous reaction; she was shakier .There were days when she could hardly *stop* shaking, and she was even more afraid of thunderstorms.

For me, it was the nightmares.

Early December,1917

Very slowly, I turned in bed, willing my straw mattress not to crunch and crackle like it always did when the straw was fairly new, but it was no use. Pa heard me. Shivering, I held my breath, waiting for the increasingly common explosion to happen. I could feel it in the air. One heavy step. Two heavy steps coming closer. Then, the inevitable growl. Maria, my newly married sister, had told me not to call it a growl. It was only the morning voice of an unhappy, hurting man. But to me, that made no sense. A growl was a growl, and when Pa hollered up the ladder to the loft's trap door, "CHILDREN! I called you once, and I don't call anyone more than twice. NOW GET!" I hesitated no more. I moved. Pa never waited for answers, just action. And I was the first one down, in the dark and in the cold, ready to do my share of work before trudging off to school.

It was going to be a long, hard winter. Somehow, I knew it. I could almost feel it in my very bones, like Ma would say. *So cold already and it's only the beginning of December.* And I'd over-heard too much. In the ramshackle house that happened rather easily. Even parents had no privacy. Once more, there would be no gifts for Christmas, unless peanuts counted, Pa had said with that deep vibrating sound, a half snort and a half chuckle, coming from somewhere in the basement of his throat. And if Ma would get well enough, she might cook up some taffy. Even through the cracks, I had heard the longing in Ma's whisper. It had saddened me. But then, when Ma was less than well, almost anything could sadden me.

Blowing at the fire that was slow in getting started, my thoughts whirled faster than I did. They always did that in the morning. *And I'll be lucky, very lucky, if I get an orange for my birthday, like last year. That had been a nice surprise and most unexpected, coming from Pa. The local storekeeper had brought in a wooden crate full of oranges to sell. That may have looked like a lot but wasn't nearly enough for the community. Pa had bought three. One for himself, one for Ma, which she promptly shared with all her at home children, and one for me because my birthday was right the next day. I shared my orange with no one unless you count the tidbit I gave Bernhard .It's*

22

not every day I got a coat of many colors, and I didn't care that my brothers were jealous. Still, I wish my birthday wasn't right before Christmas. Isn't that a dumb time to have. . .

There was clatter at the door. *Are they really finished with the milking and all their chores already? The porridge is only half cooked yet and the lunch buckets. . .*

My fingers flew as I cut the bread. At least that was co-operating with me today and not falling into a zillion pieces as it sometimes did. Generously, I spread lard on it. Five school children. Five sandwiches. Two syrup pails, one for me, and one for the boys. As I set them in order, I checked the porridge once more. It was ready to go and burned only just a trifle. I had made it. By the time everyone was sitting at the table, I was ready, too. My breathing felt a little ragged, but it's worth hurrying, I told myself. Anything is better than a scolding.

When all the heads around the table were raised in perfect unison after the silent moment of thanks that happened before every meal, and during which you could have heard a pin drop in the stillness, my little brother Bernhard who sat across the table from me winked at me. Or should I say he tried to? I saw a happy sparkle in his eyes, of that I was sure. *Was he just having a good day? Or did he mean to tell me something special?* Who cares? He may be just a preschooler yet, but he made my day.

Even as we trudged along the rough, rutty, snow covered mile and three quarter road to school, and my brothers made it plain that they would walk ahead of me – not *with* me, I was undaunted. *Somebody knows that I live. Somebody cares.* I began to hum the tune of the new song the teacher had taught us, was it already a month ago? And when my cousin came panting and puffing after me, trying to catch up, I turned around and smiled.

Chapter Two

—∽∞∽—

The day Mr. Reimer beckoned me with the gentle crooking of his finger, to come and talk with him, was an unsettling one. And of all things, it was about my predicament.

I'd been frustrated repeatedly; I had struggled over and over, but I had not discussed this with anyone. I thought nobody noticed and nobody cared, and that was just the way life was going to be. I might as well learn to be stoic and brave.

"I have noticed your problem, Tina," he told me kindly. "I have seen you squint more and more when you read – that one eye especially. I have noticed you moving closer and closer to the blackboard even when my print is large. You need glasses, and you need them *now*, before you ruin your eyes. If you don't get them, your eyes could go awry, and I mean badly. . . badly."

I stared at him for a moment and then looked down at my shoes. No way could I answer that. Or dare let him see that if I tried I would cry.

"Do you think you could talk to your parents? I know a doctor who can check your eyes and figure out exactly what kind of glasses you need. And it doesn't cost much – only a few dollars," he continued.

"I . . . uh. . . no . . . could *you* ask them? I mean, you'd have to ask Pa," I finally blurted.

It was Mr. Reimer's turn to stare at me, wordless for a moment. I got the feeling that he shared my pain, understanding me deeper perhaps than I had imagined.

Slowly he nodded his head. "I'll try," he said.

Was he really going to do it? I was not convinced, but I shouldn't have doubted him. The very next day being Saturday, he showed up at our doorstep with his team of horses. He'd made a special trip.

I was terribly curious but also embarrassed, wishing I could somehow disappear. Being the center of attention was not my idea of fun. But I needn't have worried. The men talked by the well house, out of earshot.

About half an hour later, out of the corner of my eye, watching sneakily from the kitchen window, I saw Mr. Reimer shuffle back to his team of horses. His shoulders sagged and his face looked solemn; too solemn. He did not turn to smile and wave as he usually would have.

Pa did not come in right away, but when he did, he stared at me for a minute before plunking himself heavily into his chair. He had a glum, grouchy look on his face which continued for the rest of the day. I never asked and I never found out exactly what had transpired between them. I sort of figured it out though. That night, when we were supposedly all sleeping, I heard Pa whispering loudly to Ma in what sounded to me like an accusing tone of voice. I didn't get it all, but the one line that I heard most distinctly, I will never forget. "He should have known better than to think we had money. And for glasses yet, of all things."

The hurt of that disappointment was harder perhaps on Mr. Reimer than on me at that stage. My hopes had not been unduly raised, and I did not understand the gravity of my situation as my teacher saw it. That would come soon enough.

For now, Mr. Reimer merely looked at me sadly when he saw me squint and struggle to read, while I tried gallantly to ignore the issue.

Pa, however, nursed the thing, like one might hold a grudge. He seemed to be watching me closely and Mr. Reimer even closer. All of a sudden the man could do nothing right.

One day, when we children came filing in at the end of a school day, Pa greeted me gruffly. "So, what did he try and get you to do today?" I detected a hint of suspicion and recoiled at the thought. In my opinion, Mr. Reimer could do no wrong and nobody's snide remark would topple him off that pedestal.

A few days later, my world as I had known it came to an end. "You are old enough," Pa said calmly, firmly, to me that night. "You may go to school tomorrow, one more day, but that's it. You are old enough to stay home and help Ma."

I started sputtering a retort but before the words fully formed, I scrunched them back. Both he and Ma knew very well that I loved school and wanted to go as long as possible and that this desire was the latest thing among my peers, too. We were joining hearts to fight back at the inevitable next step - being held back by struggling hard-working parents. It was also our way of saying we longed to upgrade ourselves by getting *educated.*

Ma didn't appear enthusiastic about this turn of events. No doubt she'd appreciate my help in the house but instinctively she knew my heart. She didn't argue with Pa – she almost never did that - and she never talked to me about it either. But I could feel it in her demeanour and see it in her face – if she'd had a choice, she'd have allowed me to continue.

I missed the singing and I missed the teacher.

I missed school and everything it held for me.

The only books we had at home were my parents' Bibles – they each had one, Ma's tattered Bible Story booklet, an old Catechism, and of course, the big black Gesangbuch. Everything was in German and held little appeal to me. Even if it had, all this was off limits except for Sunday afternoons – sometimes.

And I missed, perhaps more than anything else, my friends and the feeling of camaraderie that goes with being in school.

There was *one* consolation though. Without this, I doubt I could have survived. My friend Gertie had been taken out of school also, like me, in the middle of the year. But we were allowed to visit each other. After chores, of course, and walking the whole two and a half miles, but that didn't deter us. Those visits were worth the effort. They felt like a beacon of light in an otherwise cloudy sky.

Going out to meet each other on the road was a big part of the fun. Or sometimes, walking each other back and forth, again and again. That road time was often the only respite we had from the clamouring of our many siblings and the host of jobs awaiting us.

"What have you brought?" I called out to her one day, before I could see it clearly. *Gertie was carrying what?*

Happily, she waved the something in the air, and then I knew - our precious scribblers. I hurried to my under-the-bed box and dug mine out, too. We started singing through the songs, the *modern* English songs that Mr. Reimer had taught us and we had copied oh so carefully.

My favourite remained my favourite.

Keep on the sunny side,
Always on the sunny side,
It will help you every day
It will guide you all the way . . .

I saw out of the corner of my eye that Ma was listening. The pleased look on her face made me happy. But deep down in my heart, I struggled, like I always had, with the meaning of those words. *When bad things happen, how does a person keep on the sunny side of life? Like my narrow escape just the other day, at least it felt like a narrow escape, from that fellow's' naughty scheming? Or my having had to quit school before I was ready? Or Mr. Reimer's grave concern about my eyes, of which implications I had discussed only with my two best friends?*

On my very next visit to Gertie's house, she came running out to meet me, like usual, and then stopped short and stared, right in my face. What in the world was wrong with her?

She stared for a moment and then screeched, "It has happened. It has happened, just like Mr. Reimer worried."

"What do you mean?' I had noticed nothing unusual, but then we seldom used the broken little mirror at our house, and I had no idea how I looked at the moment.

Obviously feeling panicked and upset, she tried to explain. "Your eye has gone wrong. Your bad eye is poking out sideways. It looks awful."

I shivered as vibes of horror sought to envelope me, slinking up and down my spine. *Could this really be happening? Were Mr. Reimer's worst fears actually coming true?*

"I'll get my Ma's mirror and you can see for yourself," she continued.

It didn't take long for me to see the truth of her words. Luckily, she was still holding the mirror. I would have dropped it when I slumped to the ground and began to weep uncontrollably. I hadn't done such a thing for years and never in front of my friend, but this was big stuff. She was patient with me though and may have even wiped a few tears of her own.

Eventually, I got up. Our visit was over before it properly started, and I turned to leave for home. There, I could struggle without being watched. There, I would begin the process of grieving my loss. I was sure that nothing would ever feel right again.

She walked with me, slowly, slouching, like me. We were kicking up pebbles as we walked, but neither of us said a word. *After all those tears, what was there left to say?*

Gertie stopped. She was ready to go back but seemed to be stalling for words, needing to say something. Suddenly, she blurted it out, "The worst part of this is now none of the nice guys will ever, ever want to marry you."

Really? I hadn't thought of that. Not yet.

Her words got etched into my brain and would remain there for a long, long time.

Is Peter one of those guys who'd be turned off? I had already in my childish dreamy sort of way picked out the guy I hoped to marry some day. Peter was a handsome young man, way out in Blumenort, upcoming brother-in-law to my newly-aspiring-to-get-married sister. When I'd met him, it felt like he liked me, at least a little, in spite of my tender age.

I was way too young to think about such things, I knew, but Gertie was little older.

Would her fears come true in my life just like Mr. Reimer's so obviously had?

Chapter Three

———∞∞∞———

1919

*P*a had never been strong since the day of the lightning strike. He could work – sort of - but always struggled with exhaustion, dizzy spells, headaches, and chest pains. That is why, as Ma had explained to us on numerous occasions, we needed to be extra patient with him, even when he was moody. It was not without reason. And we tried to honour that request. Truly, we tried.

Now that I was home from school, I saw a side of him I hadn't noticed before. He would get out his Bible and spend time quietly reading it; spent time quietly praying, too, at the kitchen table, while the rest of us were doing the housework and stuff. In our tiny house, there was no room for privacy, even for him. When he got up from his quiet time, there was a look of peace on his face and the words that flowed out of his mouth were gentle and kind. I enjoyed that side of him so much more than the gruff side.

It was tragically short lived.

Throughout these last two years, he'd had frequent bouts of illness where he'd stayed in bed for some time. Once it was for forty days while the only food he could keep down was little swallows of milk. But then, he'd get better, not totally, but some-what. The dizzy spells still haunted him, and he shivered a lot, but he also managed to work some around the yard and with the farm animals that he loved. We had come to think that this was how life was going to be – he might not be strong, but he would always get better.

This time he did not.

On May the 9th, he passed away quietly, peacefully in his own bed, while Ma was tending to him and several of us children were hovering nearby.

I never liked to recall that sad, sad time with the funeral and all, so we won't go there. Suffice to say, it was hard. Ma was left alone with thirteen children – three were already married, but ten still needed to be raised to various extents. Bernhard, the youngest, was six. And Ma had not a dollar to her name.

I was a child going on twelve, thrust into an adult world where I did not fit. *Do twelve year olds ever fit?* Regardless, life offered no options, and so it was.

*   *   *

I learned.

Keeping busy is always a good thing, they say, and there was no lack of opportunity on that front. There was more than enough to do.

I learned to be happy. I mean . . . to appear happy outwardly.

My personal pain – the horror of losing my former reasonably good looks to one hopelessly crossed eye - had gotten harshly tossed out. I never told anyone how I spent hours trying to fix that eye, in front of the broken little mirror under the slope of our loft's roof. And how all the efforts in the world – the stretching, the twisting, the blinking, the shaking, and the praying, yes, even the praying – hadn't helped. Nothing helped. Absolutely nothing. *How can one eye suddenly be so stubbornly bad?*

But this pain had been overshadowed so quickly, so horrendously, by the greater tragedy of losing Pa, that it pretty much got lost in the shuffle. People, like the family, had "oohed" and "ahed" a lot right at first but in view of the larger picture had quickly accepted the inevitable and moved on as if it were nothing.

I ended up scrunching the tragedies together into one and hiding them carefully in the darker corners of my soul, where I wouldn't be compelled to look at them. *Don't talk about them, try not to even think about them; just leave things undisturbed.* The advice I gave myself is what I followed. It was the easiest path. What I needed to do was live life as it was and practice the art of being content. If I worked at that long enough and hard enough, perhaps one day it would become real.

That process might have gone smoother, easier, had it not been for one powerful deterrent - the absolutely brutal teasing I endured from my peers and their various buddies. The most debilitating of these blows seemed to be the indirect ones, the kind that come dribbling down the line, where somebody told somebody some snide remark about my eye and somebody tells me. Even Peter, the boy of my dreams, had been caught making hurtful comments. That *stung.*

In the meantime, I had some amazing distractions. The term 'bundles of joy," as I soon discovered, was not an exaggeration. I learned to love them.

At the time of Pa's death, there were two grandchildren. My sister Justina had a little boy named Jacob, who would be two in July. This family, the Kroekers, lived in the Morris area, so I had never connected closely with them. I'd just turned nine when she married, and my memories were vague. And to keep up a relationship, from near-Kleefeld to near-Morris by horse and buggy, well that's a long way.

Maria, on the other hand, had married Jacob Friesen and settled nearby. They had a one year old toddler named Frank and were expecting their second in August. These little ones became a real treat to me, and I did my part to help spoil them.

The big exciting news of the year though had a slightly different twist. My brother Peter and his short but lovely and energetic wife Anna had been married for five years now, and they had no children. Not yet. Too young to understand but old enough to catch the chatter, I wondered how all this would work out.

Exactly two months after Pa's funeral, one morning Peter and Anna came bouncing on to our yard in a borrowed car, of all things. Nobody in our family or in the immediate vicinity owned a car yet, but in the Steinbach area there were quite a few around already. The gleam in both of their eyes, the sparkle and the excitement, was unmistakeable. What it was about I could not imagine.

"It's working," Peter called out exuberantly. "It's happening."

"What's happening?" I hollered back and half a dozen gaping mouths behind me confirmed the question. *What indeed?*

"We are going to have a baby. A real live baby. A little girl. Can you believe it?"

No, we couldn't. My brother was considered a bit of a blabbermouth sometimes, but he had done a fine job of keeping his mouth shut on this one. It must be Anna's doing. Now, between the two of them, the story spilled out. After accepting the fact that they couldn't have children, they'd decided to adopt. It took them on a bit of a journey to find the right connections, the right numbers and addresses, to make that special application and get it all approved.

"But it's going to be worth it!" Peter beamed. "Yesterday, when the phone call came to Steinbach and someone delivered it to us, hmm, I could hardly believe it. But hey, we better get moving, Anna. We can't be late."

Late? Peter? He'd never been late once in his life yet, and he wouldn't start now.

Numb with shock – a happy kind of shock, this time - we stared after the cloud of dust that followed them in the distance. *Who would have guessed?*

And when, only a few hours later, they returned, more sedately this time but still beaming, all nine of us that were at home that day surged forward like one united little army. This we had to see.

The baby in Anna's arms was beautiful. Without a doubt the most beautiful in the world, biases not withstanding. They named her Elizabeth, after Ma. And Anna had all the clothes ready, beautiful hand made things and blankets, too. More than she needed on this hot July day.

I loved the little darling right there and then, but something made me sad at the same time. They lived in Blumenort, and I wouldn't get to see her nearly often enough.

As a distraction from the harsh realities of life, we couldn't have been given a better gift. Life might not come on a silver platter, but it does serve up some wonderful treats.

* * *

A year later, my sister Lies and my brother Abram got married both in one day. A momentous day that was and pretty perfect, too. Except for one thing. *Peter never saw me, never even looked my way.*

This turned out to be a big step into the next stage of my life – my youth, my years of young womanhood, which I feared at times would last forever. I was the only girl left - among all the boys - and I quickly became Ma's sole care-giver.

Things kept changing in our home. People who were set to help Ma - and the church was seriously in to that - would come up with their great solutions. Good men, appointed by the church with the specific job of helping widows, would come regularly to check things out and offer answers. They brought us bags of flour and sugar several times. More often though, they planned, and pretty soon I caught on to the planning. They found homes for the boys that were old enough to quit school, around the age of eleven or twelve, or sometimes maybe thirteen, but not yet old enough to make it on their own. This system was meant to solve several problems. There was one mouth less to feed for Ma, one less son to discipline or guide. In the meantime, the now fatherless boy would learn to work as well as occasionally earn a few dollars, which in turn he must give quickly to his widowed mother who he was obliged to help support. All in all, this was a good solution, we were told.

How the boys felt about it, they were never asked, and they didn't say until much later.

How Ma felt about it, well she was never asked either. Only the wet stains on her pillow and the muted sobs in the night owned up to the untold side of her story.

I was glad I was a girl. I didn't need to worry about being handed out. Actually, in the end, my youngest brother didn't either, perhaps simply because he was the baby.

But life went on. We got through it. Most of my brothers and sisters married young. Pretty soon, the baby population mushroomed. Having big families was the thing of the day. As the babies came one after the other, I fell in love with each one and became their favourite babysitter. When the crowd of little juniors got bigger, like on Sundays after church, it was over-whelming sometimes, but I was determined to make things work. In the process, I don't know who I spoiled more, my little nieces and nephews or their parents. We had a love affair going from all sides.

As the months turned into years, I tried to support Ma as well as I could. There were times my heart almost broke with the sad-ness of it. One time, I walked into the house from the garden, just after Ma had, what I'd hoped was a nice neighbourly visit from a friend. I found her bent over a box and a pile of clothing, sobbing. Obviously, she had not expected to be caught.

"What's wrong, Ma? What's wrong?'

Bravely, she tried to calm herself. "She . . . she said, the clothes weren't much but . . . but . . . but for a poor widow they would do . . . they'd be just fine." I followed her glance down to the pile on the floor and began to see what she saw. Mostly underwear. Old, lumpy, grungy stuff. Everything was patched and repatched and repatched again, worse than our rag box. Who in their right minds would wear such things, much less give them away? In the name of charity? *They'd be just fine for a poor widow?*

Sometimes, the tough moments turned out funny. Like the day Ma was sick in bed with the flu and we noticed there were visitors coming. "Hurry, Tina," she said, "put a clean sheet over my bed." In my attempt to hurry, I accidentally spread the clean sheet too far so it covered her face as well. She growled in pro-test. "Are you preparing me for the grave already? " As I quickly pulled it back, trying to correct my mistake, our eyes met and suddenly there evolved a twinkle of laughter between the two of us. By the time the company was inside, all was well.

I could go on and on with details. There are so many sto-ries to share. Like when Peter and Anna adopted their second child. Another girl. They named her Helena. She was even more beautiful than the first, if such a thing were possible.

Not long after my brother Jacob got married, he decided to build a Granny house for Ma on his yard on his little farm in Kleefeld. That was such a wonderful thing. Only Bernhard and I actually lived at home by that time. All three of us loved the idea and the house. It was one of those true God-sends. In it the three of us - Bernhard, Ma and I - bonded even more than we already had before.

Tragedies of one kind or other kept finding us, too, though. My oldest sister, Justina, was hit hard – harder than any of us. Three times within comparatively few years she lost a child. In 1919, it was baby Anna who died the same day she was born. In September of '21, it was her precious toddler, Elisabeth, who died of a sudden harsh fever or flu; in '26, it was one of her twins – Helen (twin of Peter) - who succumbed to a similar fate.

Then in a double tragedy, on the fifth of January in '28, she herself died at home in her bed while giving birth. Her infant son died with her. It was awful, I was told. Maybe it was a good thing I hadn't been there as I had originally planned.

Since her husband David had already been having a really tough time, this devastation hit very hard. Their four living children were given away to be raised by their uncles, split between Peter and Anna and Jacob and his wife. Jacob and his wife, like Peter and Anna, could not have children of their own, so they accepted this as a gift. (Later, they also adopted a child through the Agency in Winnipeg – a cute little boy named Peter.) By the time all the dust had settled, Justina's children ended up being raised in loving homes within the family circle, and that was a really good thing.

Both Abram and Isaac had the misfortune of having their wives turning ill, by turns it seemed, to the point that they needed to be hospitalized for a long time. There were a number of young children involved, so those were very challenging times. I ended up helping out a lot and the silver lining behind that was the bonding that happened between us – those children seemed to love and appreciate me forever.

For me personally, a really hard moment came when sister Lies came for a visit and told me among other things that her brother-in-law Peter was getting married. We had never really had anything going between us, him and me, other than my dreams. But a remnant of those – childish as they must have been, all based on little perhaps insignificant things - must have been tucked away in my heart somewhere and the ripping out of it felt like a tragedy. A tragedy that had started the day I lost my eye; now, it was simply the last straw.

I cried quietly in my pillow that night. As if I had had yet another funeral.

Will Gertie's predictions really come true? Will no nice guy ever want to marry me? Will I have to get old just caring for others and never have anyone to call my own?

The other questions on my mind that night were even weightier. What would I do with the soul question of the day? I so longed for clarity and peace from God. Would getting baptized be the right thing to do at this time? Would it help?

And how was I to sort out the comments from sister Maria? Her husband's cousin, she said, had expressed interest in me and might be looking for an answer. *Yea, really.* I didn't know the guy at all. And from what little I did know, I was definitely *not* interested.

Chapter Four

—◦◦◦—

$\mathscr{S}$ome of the things that were happening to me were good. Very good, in fact.

I had gone through tragedy and personal loss, and although I had never actually discovered a *correct* way of coping with such things, God had somehow been there for me, guiding me even when I least knew it. Like Peter in the Bible, I'd been scared by what felt like ghosts in my life but turned out to be like Jesus, beckoning me toward Himself. Looking back, I feel like I have walked through a desert, years of desert perhaps, but am emerging with a song of victory on my lips. Where that came from, God knows better than I do.

All the events and the emotions I went through were very real. But I had to learn to hold tight to the fact that nothing can touch us without passing through God's sifter. And if that is true, everything that happens has a purpose. It's just that I might not know it for awhile.

My search for peace is only one such example. I was floundering inwardly, clinging desperately to my faith, small as it was, and yet wondering profoundly whether what I had was the real thing or not.

I had gone for a walk, hoping to visit my friend. Finding out that she was not at home, I turned around, disappointed, wondering what I should do next. At that moment there was the rattle of a car approaching. It turned out to be Mr. Friesen, one of the preachers in our church. My favourite one, too. He was taking his newly acquired car for a leisurely ride all by himself. Why? Maybe he was just becoming familiar with his new car. It was, after all, his first.

Mr. Friesen stopped and invited me to step inside, and he'd take me to wherever I needed to go. I hesitated. I was not in the habit of riding in newfangled cars or going out with anybody for that matter – not even well-intentioned preachers. Yet, if this would give me a chance to ask questions, hey, it might be worth getting out of my comfort zone. I climbed in to the backseat.

Almost immediately, he asked, "So how's it going with you these days?"

Sometimes, I am shy, but this time, I somehow bypassed that. Before I knew it, I spilled out my whole story, my angst, my questions, some of my longings. And he turned in, in front of Ma's house, unashamed and unhurried. He took time to answer my every concern and gave me more insight into a Christian's relationship with God than anyone had ever done before.

Making *sure* of our salvation was important, and one *can* be sure, he said. I stared at him. I had never heard that before. But he was thoroughly convinced and explained it very carefully. Trusting, learning to simply *trust,* was another key issue on his heart. It made sense. Something clicked inside of me.

That unscheduled conversation catapulted me into the new peace I found by trusting Jesus more explicitly. And this led me to being baptised upon the confession of my faith, which turned out to be one of the most joyous days of my life and something I sang about a lot.

*   *   *

The question my sister Maria posed regarding a possible boyfriend intrigued me at first. What woman doesn't crave the attention of a man in her life? Yet, the more I thought about it, the clearer it became; Jacob's cousin did not fit my dream of a man. The struggle was short. I was not interested, period. I told her that but then added, "Tell him, for now, the answer is no."

Why did I leave the door open to doubts again? Saying "For now." I hate doubting and I chided myself about that. Yet, I didn't go back to change it.

"Just forget it and go on," I told myself firmly. And that's exactly what I did.

* * *

Bernhard had become a most beloved brother. Perhaps this was due to his not having been forced to leave home in his teens like the others did. Perhaps it was also due to the fact that we'd had similar experiences about finding peace in the Lord. Perhaps it was due to the fact that he wasn't getting into trouble like some of our brothers had done.

One of my brothers married a girl from a different background than ours, who already had a child – an illegitimate child from an earlier relationship. In the end, we all agreed to forgive and love and accept. Still, for quite some time, that had been a really hard nut for Ma to crack . . . . and a struggle for me, just to watch.

One of my brothers lived wild for a while and fathered a child in the process in a relationship that he did not wish to pursue. He repented but then chose to hush up the story, and as far as I know, never took ownership of the child in any way. We agreed to forgive him and even helped hush it all up, but what a blemish to live with. . . and the poor child. *Ach . The poor child.*

Some of my brothers could be temperamental and moody like Pa had been at his worst.

I would work at forgiving them quickly and being patient, like I'd been taught, but it was hard sometimes. When I suspected that one of my brothers might be abusive to his children – the children I loved - that was hard for me to digest.

Bernhard was never like that. He was God's gift of peace and blessing that both Ma and I cherished.

However, the day he came in to announce jubilantly that he was ready to go buy a car was a shocking one for Ma. She should have seen it coming I'd think. A lot of our people had been starting to buy cars. Why not us?

"What do you mean? You can't be serious?" she queried, shaking her head in disbelief.

"Yes, I am," he said firmly. For a moment, I wondered if this could escalate in to a first all-out clash between mother and son. Both of them could be stubborn.

I needn't have worried. "I have been dreaming about this for a long time, and I have saved up the money,' he explained as he took out the stash of bills from his overalls pocket to prove it to us. Even I was impressed. I knew he worked hard and was very frugal, but really?

That car became our pride and joy. Yes, I know, our tag, being branded so to speak as the children of *the poor widow* might always remain and yet, slowly but surely, we were climbing out of that image. The car gave us a big boost forward.

Bernhard, as he found time, took pleasure in escorting us around, either Ma or me or both of us. To church, to town, to visit relatives. And he even let me learn to drive it. I did that, several times, just short distances, and it was fun.

And then came the next big surprise. I couldn't believe my ears at first.

"Let's plan a trip with the car," he told me quietly one evening. "Why don't you and I go and visit our relatives in Kansas?"

Really? I had never even dreamed of such a thing. "How could that work? It would take us days to get there, and who would pay for all the gas and food and. . ."

He stopped me short. "I have the money for gas, and you could pack us a huge picnic basket full of food, and oh yes, we'd offer someone else a ride, too. Maybe cousin John would go along and help pay for the expenses."

Ma was leery at first, but she backed off quickly when she saw the eager glint in Bernhard's eyes. Almost before we knew it, the dream was no longer a dream.

It had converted to reality and would become one of the biggest adventures of our lives.

And what a trip that was! Two and a half days one way. We stopped for the nights, courtesy of John. Luckily, inn rates were low. On the way there, we ate all the food. I had brought a jar each of canned meat and fish and Plumi Moos*, bread and butter, Schnetki*, reishe tweiback*, cookies, even a rhubarb pie, my favourite. On the way home, we'd have to buy food.

Our relatives received us with wide open arms. "What a pleasure to see you," Aunt Mary beamed. And the cousins were great. They weren't like us at all. There was nothing shy or conservative or backward about them. Their church apparently had different rules than ours, too. Everybody's clothes and hairdos seemed much more modern, and the singing in church was like the forbidden songs in my scribbler. No black Gesangbuch here. Wow!

Their attitude was so warm-hearted and friendly; it over-ruled everything else. Not only did they open their lovely big homes to us and served us full course meals, they took us around to show us things. We visited, sang, and played with the children and just had a great time. In the end, they showered us with gifts, some to take home to Ma, of course. But some were for us.

Mine I cherished forever. One of my cousins gave me a lovely necklace; actually, a string of fine pearly white beads interspersed with tiny spots of gold, all bedded on a layer of white fleecy fabric and packed in a pretty blue and white paper box. As it turned out, I never got to wear that. At first, it was too precious and then it was . . . Never mind. I'm getting ahead of myself.

One gift was a lovely delicate gold rimmed fine china serving bowl which my daughter still uses.

And there was the bone china cream and sugar set with a tray. It had a lovely floral design on it with golden edges. I was convinced I had never even seen dishes nearly that beautiful. Luckily, they came packed in a sturdy box. Still, I guarded them like gold. And later, I always put them at the top of my china shelves and took them out only for the most special occasions until one day years later I dropped the sugar bowl accidentally and it broke in to a million pieces. I sat and bawled my eyes out right in the middle of making a thresher man's dinner. But again, I'm getting ahead of myself.

*   *   *

Bernhard had been eyeing Anna Dueck for a while, and I knew it. Although he spent much of his time working for brother Jacob on the farm, when he was at home, he and I would often tend our animals together. We had a horse, a few cows, a couple of pigs, and a few chickens, just enough for ourselves and to share their produce in the larger family. It was during these shared choring moments that we talked best.

"Would you mind very much if I started dating Anna?" he asked me tentatively one night. "*If* she'd go with me," he chuckled.

Why would he ask *me*? I could only imagine. It had to be for the same reason he watched out for me so often. He wanted me to be alright and not be left alone, not be left in the lurch. But he was 23 after all. . .

"Of course it's alright with me," I told him without hesitation. It had to be. It had to be alright.

And it was, until I saw them together. Even then, in a way, it was all good. I liked Anna and we got along well. It was just that seeing them together stirred up a pot of emotions inside of me that I thought I had successfully squashed.

No way could I look forward to being lonely and alone for-ever. I was going on 29 and all my peers had married. If Bernard did, too, I would truly be alone. Except for taking care of Ma and helping all my many siblings with all their many children. Ach. Yeah, I loved them all, it wasn't that. But was there really nothing, nobody, out there for me personally?

One night, I began to weep, softly at first, in my pillow. The old angst was coming back full force. But then, quite suddenly, I shook myself and stopped. *This is not the path I want to go.* Did I not learn all about trusting God and knowing there is a purpose for everything under the sun? *God loves me and will show me the way.*

I stared at the ceiling, in the dark, for what seemed like a very long time. I prayed, asking God to help me, to guide me. I tried to practise the art of trusting. Nothing happened. Finally, I turned, weary and exhausted. I needed my sleep. Tomorrow would be a new day.

As I was about to doze off, a name popped into my brain. *Jacob's cousin.* Had I been too hasty that day, it seemed so long ago now, when I turned him away?

* * *

Bernhard and Anna had a lovely courting time, all of that summer and then into fall. They set their wedding date for October the 4th. That was dating longer than some did, and there were a few remarks being made about them going modern. Shucks. I didn't care. Why should anyone else?

I loved the sparkle I kept seeing in their eyes, the spring in their steps, their joy in the planning. They had so little. Temporarily, they would move into brother Jacob's granary, and then they'd see about the future. Apparently, it did not matter. They had their whole lives before them, and they'd be together. That was what counted.

Seldom if ever had I witnessed this kind of abandonment, their quiet but strong kind of passion. Something stirred inside of me. Was it envy? I hoped not. No, I decided, it was a longing to emulate that, and although I tried, I could not shake it off. Who knows? Perhaps it was even a godly kind of longing.

*   *   *

My little knot of conviction was growing bigger. I needed to turn around. But there was more. Something inside of me was changing. As longings stirred and images flashed before my eyes, a voice in my head kept whispering, "It is time. It is time."

I resisted the urge and tried to still the little voice, but it kept bouncing back at the most inopportune times. Finally, one evening, I surrendered.

I took out a piece of paper and my pen and ink and blotter. I sat down and wrote a letter; just a short one. It wasn't easy, but I did it.

Dear Jacob (Jacob's Cousin),

I believe I may have been too hasty when I said no to you through Maria.
If you are still interested, I would like to invite you to my house for a visit, and we could talk.

Sincerely,

Tina

I sealed the letter, addressed it, and hurried off to Jacob and Maria's house. Now that I was this far, I was eager to see it through. My brother-in law was at home, and suddenly, I felt shy. I approached Maria apprehensively, but she would have none of that. Immediately, shooing off the clamouring little ones, she called her husband who caught on quickly and promised to hand deliver the message the very next day. He was going to Blumenort anyway, he said.

All I could do was wait and see.

No, change that. All I could do was wait and see and trust. *God has a plan and purpose in everything that happens.*

ON

JACOB'S

SIDE

Jacob Friesen Wiebe, February 3rd, 1899 – April 3rd, 1974

Chapter One

—◈◈◈—

1909

For some days, now ten year old Jacob had been eyeing the raft that sat quietly on the edge of the swollen little creek, only a short distance from the family home. Finally, finally today he would take his chance to prove that he was a big boy, too, just like his brother Peter. It was time.

Persuading Abraham was not easy.

"You know we are not allowed to play on the water," Abraham argued with all the vehemence a sturdy, almost nine year old could muster, tugging sharply at his overall straps. For some reason that one wouldn't stay up. Oops! The button had just popped off.

"Last week, Papi himself helped us pull out the raft. And Peter had no problem steering it."

"It was easy enough," Jacob retorted.

"But the water was lower then. That was before this big rain. And besides, Papi was here to help us just in case. Peter's bigger, too, and stronger."

That's the very thing Jacob couldn't stomach. It had always been Peter this and Peter that. Never Jacob. Lately, even Abraham favoured Peter. One of these days that would have to change, and what better time than right now? Today, when Papi had gone to the city – would be gone for two days and once again had offered Peter the chance to go along. He and Abraham, together with Mami, of course, were stuck with the chores. For now, those were all done, so why not have some fun? Why not take that raft out for a little ride on the water and create their own adventure?

47

"Just a very short ride, Abraham," he pleaded. "We can do it."

Abraham's stance was softening. It *would* be fun. "Okay," he finally conceded, "but I'll go and tell Mami." He made one beeline for the house and was back just as quickly. "Mami is napping with little Anna," he reported, "So I told Tina to tell her when she gets up."

No problem, Jacob thought, but when he turned toward the house, he saw John come rushing out, full speed. *He must be hoping to get into the fray, too. I know he's a tough little guy for being not even four years old, but I can't let him come with us. No way. How do I tell him that?*

"Hey, John, "Jacob began, trying to sound kind but firm. "You sit here on the grass and watch out for us. When we are back, maybe I'll give you a ride next." Strangely, the boy co-operated and plunked himself down on the damp grass to watch.

The two boys had no problem getting onto the raft and loosening the boards that they used as paddles for steering. Everything went smoothly. Nothing scary happened.

Jacob was absolutely certain that this was his chance to prove he was more grown up than anyone gave him credit for. The slightly cool spring breeze felt good on his face. Both he and Abraham were half sitting, on their haunches, using their paddles bravely just like Peter had taught them. It all seemed so right. Even when they felt the current of the creek begin to pull them forward faster, it was all just part of the adventure.

Suddenly, Abraham said, "Let's turn back. It's time. You said just a very short ride."

Jacob nodded in agreement, and immediately, they both began working the paddles to turn the raft around to go back. That's when the first knot of apprehension pulled at Jacob's insides. The raft wasn't budging, not even a bit. It was being stubborn and ornery, refusing to be steered to the side so they could pull up to shore as Jacob had planned. Instead, it was going faster, quickly taking them downstream toward the neighbours' pasture. Jacob couldn't even feel the creek-bottom any more with the paddle, and the harder he tried to steer the clumsy raft, the more it shook and waggled as if it had a mind of its own.

Water splashed over them, and Jacob realized they'd soon be soaked to the skin.

"What are we going to do?" Abraham asked anxiously. Their eyes locked for a moment as fear wove its way through their minds. Jacob had no answers. He'd never felt so small in his life.

Once he knew they could not steer the raft, he decided the next best thing was to keep the raft from tipping and themselves from falling off; hoping they would come to a tree trunk or some other barrier they could use to save themselves. He dare not panic; thinking clearly could make all the difference. Maybe even a life and death difference. Wow! This wasn't nearly what he'd had in mind.

Very shortly, they did come to a barrier, but not one they'd have thought to ask for. They ran into a fence, of all things, apparently strung across the stream; luckily, it was not barbed wire but a sheep fence - the kind with countless little oblong sections in it. Papi didn't have one like this; it must be the neighbours'. The trouble was it appeared to be bending and pulling and stretching with the force of the raft's pushing against it. Would it hold? Could they count on it so they could use it to manoeuvre themselves to safety?

It had to be worth trying. Maybe it was an answer to the silent prayers Jacob had sent upward for help.

Gingerly, Jacob snagged his paddle into the fence; then, he told Abram to do the same. By tugging firmly and then pushing a bit and exchanging places, again and again, they very slowly edged sideways. It seemed to take forever, but it *was* working.

"Good," Jacob said. "We are out of the current now. A little further and we've made it."

Maybe in the excitement Abraham wiggled too much or maybe his paddle struck some obstacle. It was never quite clear why, but right at that moment, there was a huge splash and Abraham was in the water, headfirst. Without thinking, Jacob jumped after him and grabbed him, pulling him up fast. They were in the overflow, happily not in the creek's current any more, and very soon they both stood to their feet, feeling the wonderful solid ground beneath them. Abraham kept sputtering and spitting water for a while, shaking the water off his head, too, but Jacob refused to let him go until he'd led him safely to dry land.

The raft? Surely somebody would take care of that - on a different day, no doubt.

For now, all that mattered was getting home safely and before both of them caught their death of a cold.

*   *   *

Several things turned out in Jacob's favour. Little John had gotten concerned and ran in to call Mami. She had come running to check on his story and met them while they were coming in all shivering and soaking wet. Yes, she was upset - of course, but not as badly as she might have been. Relief was the big thing, it appeared. Indeed, explaining this episode to their father would have been a challenge had their adventure turned out any worse than it did.

Papi's homecoming, too, was tempered by goodwill. Jacob *knew* for a fact that he would get the threshing of his lifetime once Papi heard. *It never happened.* Pa seemed to be looking hard at him a lot for the next few days, but that was pretty much the end of it. They never even talked it out.

Sniffles notwithstanding, neither of them got sick either; not really sick, that is. Abraham snapped back so fast it was amazing. And Jacob, well he was glad it was him because the whole thing *was* his fault; he developed a nagging cough that hung around for a while.

Perhaps the biggest thing was the twist that happened to his intentions. He had wanted so badly to prove that he was big. Instead, he felt like he'd grown smaller than ever; yet in that very process, he had shown remarkable maturity and accomplished perhaps more growing up in one day than he could have in a year of yearning.

One thing did not sit in his favour unless there was a reason that only God could see. For as long as Jacob lived, he would always be haunted by swollen creeks or even overflowing ditches sometimes. They would never again be *anybody's* playground - neither would rafts - not as long as *he* had something to say about it.

*   *   *

Jacob checked out his report card again. It looked good. Everything – all three of the needed subjects – Reading, Arithmetic and Schoenschreiben,* showed he'd done good work. Very good work. His efforts had paid off.

Arithmetic came natural to him. Most of that subject he could have done in his sleep and still called it fun. Reading? That took a little more diligence now that the words were getting bigger, but still, he'd worked hard and he'd made it. But Schoenschreiben*? He used to be lousy at that. Without discussing it with anyone, he had practised endlessly. He wanted so badly to excel in the things he did. Finally, it was making a difference.

Would Papi be pleased?

*   *   *

It was suppertime. His sister Tina had said so because Mami had just said so. Everyone had come filing in, detouring first, of course, to the wash basin that sat on a bench behind the house and sharing the large, predominantly grey towel that hung on the brass hook beside it.

They found their places around the sturdy, homemade wooden table. Everybody had their spots – always. Papi sat at the end, the head. On the behind side of the table, on a long lighter-brown wooden bench, sat all the boys, as soon as they were old enough. First was John, still three at the moment but acting more like four, sturdy, energetic, aggressive. He was sort of strong-willed and could throw a good tantrum. but in Papi's presence. that happened only once. Then came Abram, the adorable one whom everybody called cute. His eyes often sparkled with joy and laughter – that's just who he was. He was more talkative, too, than some of his brothers. Next came Jacob. He was the quietest one of the bunch, and for some reason, he seemed to keep falling between the cracks. Maybe because he was a middle child or maybe because he was a late bloomer, whatever that meant, or maybe, heaven forbid, there was something wrong with him. He had never dared ask, and no one had ever thought to answer his nagging questions.

Then, of course, there was Peter, the oldest, Papi's namesake and almost always his pride and joy: he was going to be 12 in fall.

On the front side of the table sat Mami, in a smaller brown wooden chair. To her left, at Papi's end, sat two year old Anna, still in a baby chair. She was chubby and round faced and loved to laugh when Jacob played with her. He liked that a lot. On the other side of Mami sat 7 year old Tina, Mami's namesake, also on a chair - there had to be some benefits to being a girl. She was slender and not very big for her age, sort of shy, too, but smart and an excellent helper in the house.

The spots that would be filled later by David and then baby Frank would come soon enough, but let's not get ahead of ourselves.

Conversation around the table was kept to a minimum as everyone dug in to the large pan of fried potatoes, the fresh peas from the garden, the canned farmer sausage, the home-made bread. The butter hole may have been at Papi's end, but he was good; he always let everybody share his butter. "There's enough for all of you," he'd say, unlike some fathers Jacob knew.

Today, Jacob, like so many times before, was in a reflective mood. Deep thinker that he was, he didn't need to talk to enter-tain himself; his thoughts kept him sufficient company. And yes, they were good, mostly good thoughts this time.

He was proud of his father. Papi was an excellent horseman who could train and control even the wildest horse in no time. Papi ran the farm like a business, ahead of the times, and pros-pered. Everyone knew that. He was on the boards that ran the community, in church, in school, and in the village, and people respected him for that. He respected himself, too. And he wasn't poor either, like some of their neighbours; nor was he slothful and sloppy looking like one of their friends or sickly and slow like one of their relatives. Jacob knew he had every valid reason to be proud of his father.

And Mami, too. She may be short and chubby, but did that matter? She was an excellent cook. Jacob liked almost every-thing she made – the bread she baked, the meat and fish and preserves and veggies she canned, the cakes and cookies and pies she made. Even her carefully churned butter. And her

Plumi Moos* was out of this world. It all helped balance out the fact that she seemed moody at times - or might she be sad about something? And sometimes a wee bit cranky? Should he not have admitted that? Maybe he just needed to understand her better. Perhaps there was a reason. On more than one occasion, he had heard someone say it's too bad she lost yet another one. *We have never had a baby that died.* What could they have been talking about?

And looking around the table, he reminded himself; he could be thankful, too, for his brothers and sisters. Everyone of them was healthy and decent-looking and smart and . . . and even normal, he *hoped.*

There was only one thing, but he couldn't have said what it was, because he himself did not know. It was too vague. Something like a missing link, *something* about his family; maybe he should call it a mystery because he couldn't put his finger on it. If he could find a way to figure it out – now wouldn't that be something?

Chapter Two

—⁘⁘—

1910

*B*eing sick isn't fun. Even besides the obvious, there are disadvantages. Like having to stay in bed when you'd rather be playing, or missing out on Mami's best cooking. Why a kid would get sick in the middle of harvest time, right around the end of August, is a bit of a mystery, too.

Every once in a while, Jacob decided, he might just like the advantages he got out of it. Perhaps, for some reason, the timing had been just right. But who could have guessed that?

He had always liked Great Aunt Margreta. He had never figured out why, how they were related, or even why she was called great, but so be it. He was always full of questions, people told him. That was true, he knew, but they were questions no one chose to answer. And he'd had his fill of being frowned upon as if he should have known better. So he'd learned to zip his mouth and pretend it didn't matter. Maybe it really didn't.

When Jacob had come down with a violent case of summer sickness, Papi got worried. Perhaps his concern stemmed from the gossip saying it could be typhoid, but even after that was ruled out, the symptoms were not right, his concern didn't lessen. Perhaps it was because Jacob was sicker, weaker, and paler than he'd ever been. Or maybe it had something to do with Mami not feeling well either and needing extra care right then. Whatever the reason, one afternoon, Papi had his limit, it seemed. He climbed up the stairs himself to feel Jacob's hot forehead, trying to gage the fever, and personally emptied the pot from the latest vomit. Thankfully, there was not a huge mess to clean up.

He stood there puzzled for a little while, then his usual decisiveness kicked in. "I am taking you over to your Great Aunt Margreta," he fairly barked. "She's always offering to help us out. Yes, that's what we'll do." His voice was gruff; he sounded strangely anxious. Was he trying hard to convince himself of something?

* * *

Great Aunt Margreta lived alone in a little granny house nestled comfortably in the backyard of her daughter's home. Their children had built it for her right around the time her husband died several years earlier. Her youngest daughter had still been at home then; soon she was gone, too, though, married just like the other four. Every one of them had on more than one occasion insisted that she live with them, but she had an independent streak. As long as she was able, why not manage on her own? Hadn't she, after all, been a midwife? Hadn't she hitched up the horse herself when she needed to? Might she not still be doing that if the younger Mrs. Reimer hadn't slowly but surely taken over her work?

She didn't have a guest room, but that was no problem. She simply piled a few blankets on to her leather-covered sitting bench, added a pillow, and tucked the boy in with her shabbiest little quilt – *just in case.*

Jacob had appeared to be at the point of collapsing when his father brought him. He was being half carried, half trying to stumble along. But after Margreta had gently tucked him in, he had very quickly dozed off. And that's how it remained. For two days and two nights, that's pretty much all he did – sleeping or half sleeping and caring very little about anything else.

Margreta had always loved the boy; he was her sister Elizabeth's daughter Margaret's poor, precious baby. In the past, her sister would gladly have helped out, too, but she was getting old now and her health had been failing rapidly. Life had not been kind to her for some time. But taking care of someone during an illness came natural to Margreta. Nursing had always interested her – it gave her satisfaction like few things did. As long as there was a chance a person could get better, she would make sure it was happening. With a shelf full of remedies, a brain full of ideas, and a heart full of love, what better options could anybody find?

* * *

On the third day, Jacob awoke with a start and sat up. He shook his thick mop of hair as if needing to get rid of the cobwebs. He started getting up, but suddenly the room spun. Quickly, he slouched back onto his pillow.

"Not so fast, young man." Margreta said kindly. "You've been very ill, so take it slow." She helped him sit comfortably at the end of the bench, leaning on a pillow, tucking the quilt around him once more. She brought him a fresh glass of water. Then she warmed up the pot of chicken soup she'd made yesterday – this time, it agreed with him.

"Good thing," she told herself. "It's working. Soon, he'll be just fine."

"Is there anything else you are hungry for?" she asked after a bit.

"Yes," Jacob said. "Schnetki.* Schnetki with jam."

"Good. That's easy enough." she said as she hustled off to the cupboard to find the ingredients.

* * *

As Jacob munched on the still-warm fluffy tea biscuits, he got a brand new brain wave. *Maybe Aunt Margreta could answer my questions; now, when it's just her and me and nobody's around to call me stupid. Hmm.*

Did she think the same thing? Why else would she suddenly offer to visit? She was eating some biscuits herself. Hers she had with a cup of still-slightly-warm coffee though, not milk like she'd given him.

"You know, Jacob,' she said with that frank, honest, open look she was known for, "I've wanted to visit with you for a long time. You won't remember, of course, but you lived with me once, for four whole months, when you were just a wee little guy. You celebrated your second birthday during that time. And

56

ever since then, I have always felt you were someone special to me."

Ah, that answers one of my hundred questions. But it also posed more – many more.

"Why did I live with you?" he questioned, tilting his head sideways, squinting at her shrewdly.

"You really don't know?'

"No. How could I? Nobody's ever told me."

Margreta had sometimes suspected that; now, she knew. No wonder she'd seen that lost look on his face so often; he didn't even know who he was. Maybe his brothers didn't either, but she'd start with the one she was closest to at the moment. It was high time somebody told him the story. But just exactly where should she begin?

"Your mama. . . ." she hesitated.

"What's wrong with my Mami?"

"Nothing's wrong with your Mami. It's just . . . it was . . . not always . . . your new Mami . . . "

"What? I don't know what you are talking about? '

"Okay Jacob; let's erase everything I said and start over."

"Okay?"

"Once upon a time, your Papi was a young man. He was one of the best catches in the community. You probably know what I mean. He was smart and strong and good looking, honest and hard working, in good standing with the church. And it happened that my niece; should I add one of my very favourite nieces; she was my sister Elizabeth's second daughter and really beautiful, too. Anyway she fell in love with your Papi and he with her. You may notice sometimes that in some marriages the couple just barely manages to get along with each other, but not in their case. They loved each other with a passion that was wonderful to see. On November 1st, in 1896, right here in our church, he and Margaret were married."

"Margaret? My mother's name is Katharena, not Margaret!"

"Sh. Sh. Just wait. And listen carefully. I am telling you an important story."

"Let's go back to the young couple. They not only loved each other fiercely, but they were also both dreamers and doers. The community was just beginning to spread out from the village, as it used to be, and your Papi was eager to be one of the first to establish an individual farm of his own. And they did it, Margaret supporting him all the way. That became the farm you are still living on now. Whenever she could, she was out there helping him, building things and putting up pens and fences. She soon created a large lovely garden and planted a whole bunch of trees. She was young, yes, she turned 19, I believe it was a week after her wedding, but that didn't hold her back, even though your Papi was about six years older.

"Exactly one day after their first wedding anniversary, they had their first baby born to them. He was a beautiful child, perfect in every way. They named him Peter after your father. Everything had gone smoothly with his arrival, and they couldn't have been happier, both of them, pleased and proud."

Jacob's eyes had grown bigger, wider. He was listening very closely now. Some of that was almost making sense. Almost.

"But time went on. About a year and three months later, you arrived. This time things did not go so smoothly."

"What was wrong?"

"Well. You were a good baby and all, but there were complications, you know. Sometimes, there are. It happens. For one thing, you were not as strong and perfect as your brother had been and still is. I was there. I was the midwife. There was no other doctor around. I didn't know it right away, but later I found out that at least part of your problem had to do with Rickets."

"What's Rickets?"

"That's a disease of the bones that sometimes affects young children. Bones are softer and weaker than usual, sometimes crooked, too, and it takes a child longer to learn things like walking and running. Sometimes, the child's head seems to grow rapidly while the legs remain smaller than average until eventually they catch up."

"Do I still have that?" *Was that why he could never run as fast as his brothers when they played?*

"No, you are fine now. But it did set you back for *quite* a long time. The other thing I was going to tell you, though, is your Mama had a very rough time that day. Not because of you, one never really knows why these things happen, but for whatever reason the good Lord has in mind. And she didn't get her strength back like she did the first time."

"So, there you were. You were weaker than usual and so was she. The two of you would nap together often and became so close. It was very special – beautiful to see, actually. When you fussed, she could settle you down so fast it was unreal."

"Where was Papi?'

"He was busy farming. And taking care of Peter. They formed a special bond, too, and your Papi was very pleased with him. Peter was not only cute, but a fast learner, too, and eager to prove himself as Papi's big boy. The whole thing seemed pretty perfect for a while."

"And then?"

"I should have said, your Mami was never lazy, not once. But she wasn't well. Still, whenever she felt up to it she worked outside and helped on the farm. Even though you couldn't walk yet, she took you along and put you somewhere on a blanket. Wherever she was, you were, too. And with great effort, she planted some more trees. You know that row along the west side of your yard? She planted those all that year, and she told me they were for her children to remember her by."

Jacob frowned. "What does that mean?"

"No one knew what she meant. Only later did we figure it out."

"But that's pretty much how things went when you were little. You were a late bloomer in many ways. Your Papi was worried about that, but she kept saying you'd be fine. She really believed in you. And as we all know, she was right. But it wasn't always obvious at first. And things got worse before they got better. "

"Like how?"

"You were unusually late with learning to walk, but you crawled really well, and your Mami wasn't worried. And you didn't talk early like Peter either. But that didn't prevent your Mami from knowing what you wanted. She always knew. But then came September; time for Abraham to be born. This time, the baby was fine, but she was not. Nothing had really gone wrong as far as I could tell; still, *something* was wrong. I wished so badly I knew how to help her. But no one had any answers.

Your Papi actually took her to the city to check with a doctor, but it made no difference. One day, when I came to help for awhile, I caught them both kneeling together by the bed, praying. They had so much love, so much reason to live. Yet pretty soon, we all realized she would not be long for this world. And everyone was very sad."

Jacob stared hard at Aunt Margreta, trying to grasp every word he was hearing.

"But how she loved you all. Even lying there, so weak, in her bed. She'd nurse the new baby and then cuddle up with you, coaxing you along. You learned to walk right by her . . . her deathbed. Well, not actually, but you took a few stumbly steps that one time and she was so proud of you. And Peter was, too, and Papi. It was a happy day."

"But the happiness didn't last. On December the 15th, I believe it was, when baby Abraham was only three months old, she simply did not wake up from her nap – the nap she always had with you. She was gone. It was just a month past her 23rd birthday. Peter had just turned three. You were going on two – in February.'

Aunt Margreta swallowed hard before she continued. "That was the saddest funeral I have ever been to. Even worse than my own husband's or my little baby Susha's." And suddenly, she swiped at a stray tear; the hanky was always in her apron. "You guys had all lost so much. You boys were motherless. Your Papi had lost the love of his life. Even I . . . er . . . lost my favourite niece."

For a few moments, the two just looked at each other. Then, she whispered, "I can never erase that day from my brain. Your Papi was so-o-o heartbroken and you children so-o-o lost. There was miserable weather, too, cold and a biting north wind with stinging snow thrown in every so often, but that was nothing compared to the broken hearts."

Suddenly, as they kept staring at each other, Jacob slumped back on to his pillow and began to weep, like he hadn't for a long time. Oh, he remembered well when he used to cry, all the time, about anything. But he'd been teased a few times too often, and one day, he'd vowed to put an end to that. Forever.

Changing that had been brutal at first, but his mind was made up and it had worked. Until now.

When she had dried her own tears, and his, she tucked him in for another nap. *Had she told him too much? Too much for his tender heart? Too much for one day perhaps?*

"Sorry, if I talked too much."

Jacob simply shook his head, vigorously – *no*.

"When you are ready for more, just let me know. I'll tell you all the rest."

Margreta turned around to putter in the kitchen. Baking some sweet treats, maybe some cinnamon rolls, would be a good diversion. As she heard Jacob's sniffles gradually slow down and be replaced by deep breathing that sounded like sleep, she sighed in relief.

This had been one tough thing to talk about, but it was good for the soul, she was sure. And for the poor boy, so long overdue.

And she began to sing softly the hymn they had sung at church on Sunday. She couldn't remember all the words, but the Bible verse she'd read, was it this very morning? It had carried a similar thought. In Romans 11, if she remembered correctly, perhaps the very last verse, it had said something about all things being through Him and to Him and for Him, and He would get the glory forever, amen.

That was a thought and a comfort she could live with.

*   *   *

Quietly, Margreta shut the door behind her, careful not to drop any wood from the load on her arm. The chickens were fed, and she was ready to stoke up the fire to bake the tasty morsels she had so perfectly rolled.

The rustling behind her made her turn. Ah! Jacob was awake; not only awake, but walking toward her with a crooked hint of a smile. If she didn't know better, she could have entirely missed the tear streaks and mussed up hair, he looked that much better. He'd be fine now.

"Don't get well too fast now or your Papi will be here to pick you up before we finish our story," she challenged him. Jacob chuckled then sat down on the wooden chair by her table. He had no idea what his parents were up to or when Papi would come for him.

She was making some supper for the two of them while the stove was hot. When she pulled out the pan of rolls, steamy, hot, and heavenly smelling, everything else was ready, too. And for the first time, the two sat down for a proper meal together.

Never before, that Jacob could remember, had he ever been anywhere as the only guest and been treated as if that was special.

Jacob didn't know how to ask his questions, so he hoped Auntie would start up again. And he was not disappointed.

"So where was I?" she began. "Ah, yes, at the funeral, but we can't stay with the sorrow of that, bad as it was." She paused for a moment, perhaps organizing her thoughts. "And it's clear now, right? Your very own Mamma, whose name was Margaret, and who loved you with a passion, who loved all three of her little boys dearly but you not the least, who was the love of your Papi's heart, died when she was 23. She was buried in the village graveyard, behind the church."

"I . . . I've never been there."

That puzzled Margreta. Was their father trying to protect the boys from the reality of it, or just from the pain? Either way, she must remedy that.

"I'll take you. Now that you are getting better, we could even walk there from here. Maybe tomorrow, or soon at least."

"But back to our story. Life had to go on. Each of you boys was temporarily put into loving homes which could take care of you. I was the lucky one who got *you*. Your father would sometimes come to visit, but he was a broken man. It was the worst winter of his life."

"After a few months, he realized that he had to do something. He didn't want to, mind you. Like I said, he had really loved Margaret and had dreamed only of having a long and satisfying life together with her. But all that was gone now. And he struggled even with his faith. How can a loving God allow such heartbreaking tragedy to happen to His children?"

"Well, why does He?" Jacob would never have dared pose such a question anywhere else.

"We don't know why. Only He knows. But the Word teaches us that as the heavens are higher than the earth, so are MY ways higher than yours. And another thing it says is that God is the potter and we are the clay; and as clay, we cannot even think of telling the potter how to make us or shape us or whatever He wants to do with us. It's all His decision. Our part is to submit to Him and trust Him, even when it's hard. He sees the whole big picture, and He knows all the reasons why."

"Really?" No one had ever talked this way to him before. Everyone always seemed to think he was either too small or too ignorant to understand.

"Yes," Margreta continued as she watched him absorb her words. "But your Papi still loved you boys and wanted to give you a home again. He started looking around for a suitable woman who would make a good mother for you as well. That's when he met Katharena. She seemed agreeable; in fact, I believe she was honoured by his proposal and was pleased to become your new Mami."

"Did Papi uh . . . love her?"

"I think so. Probably not quite like Margaret, but still, yes. Your Papi is a good man; he always wanted to do things right."

"Oh."

"So they got married, later that winter, early spring, actually. You had turned two while you were with us. You were walking quite nicely by then; we had practiced a lot on that.

Your brother Abraham was about ready to start crawling, and he was really cute. All in all, it was a lovely wedding day, and we were thankful for the new feeling of hope it created for your family."

"And then they had more babies?"

" Right. First Tina, then John, then Anna. And oh, yes, your Mami has been losing some, too; several, in fact. I'm sure you know about the little grave markers behind the garden; that's where the little ones are buried – the babies that died before they were even born. Such can be a very sad and discouraging thing. They lost one last year – remember when Mami was so sick? Well, they are going to have another one any day now, and they've been quite anxious about it. Hopefully, nothing goes wrong this time."

"Ach." Why was he feeling so removed? As if he was visiting another world entirely. But his reverie was interrupted abruptly by a noise at the door.

"Hey. Your Papi is here."

Sure enough. There he stood at the door, looking weary but smiling.

"All is well?" Margreta asked.

"Yes," he said. "All is well, and it's a boy. He arrived yesterday, August 31st, and we are naming him David. And Jacob, how's he doing?'

"He was *pretty* sick, but he's coming around now. Should be fine in another day or two. Can you sit down and have a cinnamon roll with us? They're still warm."

"No thanks. I promised Katharena I'd be right back."

"Well then, make sure you drop Jacob off again when you drive by here. He and I have had a nice visit, and we're not quite done yet."

The two looked at each other solemnly for a moment. Then, Papi slowly nodded his head, and Jacob could only hope that he would remember.

Chapter Three

—·ᴥᴥᴥ·—

September 1910

Coming home had been good.

It seemed to Jacob that maybe his Papi looked at him with more respect than usual, and if that were true, it would certainly satisfy the biggest and most nagging longing of Jacob's heart. He had no time to be reflective though. School started next week and there was much to do before they'd be ready. Papi had talked of keeping Peter home to help, but at the boy's insistence, he had agreed to postpone that for a little while, maybe for a year or at least until next spring.

Inside the house, everything was different. There was a maid working in the kitchen - a cousin that Papi had hired for a few weeks to help out so Mami could get her rest.

And of course, there was the new baby – David. Since Anna was already 3 1/2, it had been a while since there was a little one in the house. Jacob liked looking at the baby and thought he was cute, but when Mami suggested he could hold the baby, he hesitated. He'd never held a baby. When she offered it again, he agreed to try and to his own amazement found that it worked and felt good. It was actually fun.

*   *   *

Jacob was surprised a few days later when Papi approached him, "I am taking the wagon; I need to go out for some business, and if you wish, you can go along. I promised Great Aunt Margreta I'd drop you off sometime soon. So you could finish your visit."

Wow! Papi had remembered. And being offered a place with Papi, as his only passenger, was a noteworthy thing. It was the first time ever as far he could remember.

Papi seemed puzzled when he looked at Jacob, but he asked no questions and Jacob offered no answers. Some things are not easy to talk about.

At Great Aunt's house, Jacob felt nervous at first, but only for a few minutes. There was something so calm and accepting about Great Aunt, it melted away his fears, and soon, they were chatting as if they had hardly been interrupted, continuing right where they had dropped things off.

"So, do you want to walk to the graveyard first or a little later?" she asked.

"Let's do it first," Jacob suggested tentatively, being a little anxious still. There seemed to be no one around who would embarrass though. Soon, he forgot all about such fears. When Great Aunt showed him the grave of his mother, they simply stood there, gazing down at the ground, quietly, for perhaps a couple of minutes.

"Your Mama was a wonderful person, and I will never forget her," she finally half-whispered in churchlike tones.

Jacob's voice was even quieter. "And I will never forget what you have told me. . . Now, I know . . . . Now, I know. . . ." and then his words tapered off to nothing.

Back at the house, she showed him her stack of syrup cookies that she had just made, the kind you stick together with jam. Tomorrow, two of her children were coming home and she needed to be ready. She offered Jacob some. As they sat together at the table, enjoying the fresh crunchy tasty little bundles, she turned to him again. "You had some more questions you wanted to ask me, didn't you?"

How did she know? Jacob had had several, he knew, but right now, he could only recall one. "When I was little, everybody always looked at me as if I was different than usual - like maybe something was wrong with me. I have always wondered why? Was it because of that er. . rickets thing or was there something else wrong or why was that?"

"Do you remember something specific?"

"Yes. I remember wetting my pants and being punished for that by having to wear a dress, a girl's dress, and I was so upset about that I got all discouraged and sad, and I guess I kept right on having the same problem, because I remember having to wear that dress forever like and hearing Papi say, 'That boy will *never* grow up.'"

"Hmm. I remember some of that. But I think I can explain it, and all of a sudden, it will make a lot of sense. You see, when you went to live at home, you had not yet learned to love your new Mami. You didn't even know her. In fact, small as you were, you had not yet gotten over your grief of losing your own Mamma. I will never forget how day after day you kept looking for her. At our house, you had already accepted her absence, but going home opened it all up again. Your mind was not slow, perhaps even smarter than average. But you and your Mama were bonded very closely, and you had an awful time accepting the fact that she was gone."

"Now, in comes your new Mami. She had never been married before, never had her own children. Suddenly, overnight she has three; two in diapers. Everything is new to her. But remember, you are two years old and fairly big for your age. She is certain that you should already be toilet trained. Maybe you should have been, maybe she was right. And that would have been my fault. I had decided while you lived with us that you weren't ready, that you had enough to deal with without pushing that. So I just left it be."

"But your Mami was determined, and the two of you butted heads. You didn't know her, didn't like her – not yet, had no desire to please her. You were still busy looking for your own Mama in your house all over again, and when that failed to bring results, you were enveloped in grief all over again. Somewhere in that process, you became an angry rebellious stubborn little two year old that was hard to handle. It became like a war between the two of you that escalated to almost everything around you and then somehow, you got stuck in that dark mode. It looked for quite awhile like you'd never get out of it. Nothing worked. I remember praying for you and yearning to help, but it was not my place. "

"Why only me and not the others??"

"Peter was older. He could talk and communicate and understand things better already. He grieved, too, but not in the same way. And Abraham? He was too little."

"Oh."

"And remember, too, that God makes each of us different. You were, like I said last time, a bit of a late bloomer anyway – that means it's supposed to take you longer to grow up in certain ways and there's nothing wrong with that, plus you were a deep thinker with strong feelings but found it hard to express those. So, your struggles raged inside of you where you couldn't get them out, and people had a hard time understanding that, young child that you were."

"So how did I ever get over it?"

Margreta chuckled. "I don't know. I just know that you did eventually. You certainly haven't been in diapers for a long time now." She chuckled again. "Maybe it was in answer to your Mama's prayers, or even mine. Maybe it was just a matter of time. Some things take time; lots of time. Or maybe, ach, we'll probably never know for sure."

"But you think I am okay now?"

"Certainly." Margreta's mood was cheerful and convincing. "You may always be a step or two behind the fastest runners, but who cares? You are you, and you will be just fine. You have every reason to be pleased with yourself, too; I heard your last report card was great in every way."

"Who told you that?"

"Your Papi."

Really? Jacob's mouth dropped open in amazement, but before he could say anything, they heard the familiar rattle of horses and wagon, and Jacob hurried off to meet his father just like he'd been instructed. But he wore a smile on his face now, a big new smile.

* * *

Christmas 1911

It was an unusual Christmas.

68

Baby Frank had made his appearance just two days before, on the evening of the 23rd. Everything went smoothly this time; nobody was ill and both Mami and the baby were doing well. Papi seemed so relieved – now that Jacob understood *why*, he felt for his father. Thankfully, this time there was no reason for concern. The baby, once again, was healthy and precious; everyone was happy.

As it turned out, Frank would become known as little Frank. He would be the baby of the family; he would always be smallest in stature no matter how hard he would try to outgrow that; but Frank would always be Frank regardless. He was easy-going and everybody loved him.

*   *   *

Jacob had been trying to learn to whistle, but somehow the sounds never came out quite right. It was as if his tongue kept getting in the way, but he kept working at it. That song he'd heard at church on Sunday – *Holy God, We Praise Your Name* - had stuck with him, and he'd love to whistle it. His brothers might have sung it; they had better voices. But for him, whistling would be the perfect achievement, if only he could learn.

"Hey, you got it. I could tell right away which song you are whistling, and you are doing good." It was Peter. And coming from his older brother, that rare compliment would be remembered for a long time.

*   *   *

1912- 1918

The day Papi told Jacob it   was time to quit school and become a man had been a hard one for him. He had actually liked school and would miss it. Even the teacher had seemed to appreciate him lately.

But the other side of it felt good. He had always wanted to prove himself; hopefully, this time around, he would not make too many foolish mistakes like he did so long ago on the creek.

With his inclination to deep thinking and planning, he felt the void though. Just physical work was not enough; he needed something to stimulate his brain and spirit. So, he began to go to church, not because it was the thing to do; he needed to satisfy his hunger. And he began to read the bible he'd gotten at school, discuss some of the portions with his brothers and friends, and all around pursue at least some of what he found there. The least he could do was to try and become a good man, he figured out, and to that end he applied himself thoroughly.

In fact, to prove yourself spiritually – in his community - that was the thing of the day. The source of your faith may well be important, but not nearly as important as the proving of it by your works. At least, that's how it came across to him. It may not be exactly that you are saved by works, but it sure was mighty close. At times, Jacob struggled with this very question; there were several bible verses that made this theory sound wrong; yet again and again, he came back to the same result. And, he eventually concluded, that would *be just fine.*

Going to church was a comparatively new experience for Jacob. As a whole family, they had attended only sporadically as long as he could remember. Papi always went. When Mami felt up to it, she joined him and usually took along one or two of the smallest children while the rest of them simply stayed at home. They had to be big and take care of themselves and each other. When Mami didn't go, Papi had begun to take one of the oldest boys. It used to always be Peter, but now Jacob was being invited, too, and pretty soon, Abraham as well. So, it had become an almost-family affair.

That was the custom; other families did things much the same way. There was no program for the children, and they were not expected to get involved with things pertaining to their faith. Not other than reading or even browsing through the little blue *Biblical Stories* every family owned and every child loved. It offered pictures, amazingly graphic and very intriguing. But a church service consisted generally of singing a few many-versed songs out of the big black Gesangbuch and two seemingly long and dry sermons in High German, which, for the greater part, were copied in scribblers and re-used many times over. It took a fair bit of maturity for a young person to actually receive a blessing out of a service.

Every church had several elected lay ministers besides the bishop who was in charge of the various churches in his district. The services were held in rotation. Each of the churches in the group hosted a service perhaps every three to five weeks, depending.

The fear of the Lord was strongly taught, as was respect for the leaders – hence, there was no room for rebellion. Not usually, at least. No one wanted to be in trouble with either God or the church. And there were some perks – very nice benefits to the system. Right after the service, it was socializing time. Almost everybody either went somewhere or invited someone over. That was fun, and the young people loved it. It was their hang out time.

As long as you have friends and can have some fun, why should you complain?

*   *   *

"Great Aunt Margreta has had a stroke," Papi announced after coming home from the village. He had taken milk to the cheese factory – still did that some days even though it was the boys' job more often now. It was one way of meeting people, of keeping tab on whatever was happening around them. "And she's not doing well."

Jacob wanted to go see her. So did Abraham and Tina. Papi exchanged a glance with Mami, whatever that meant, and then nodded. "We'll go tomorrow. Anyone who wants to can come."

That was different.

Aunt Margreta lay there in her bed, silently sleeping it looked like. Even when Jacob stood right beside the bed and touched her gently on the shoulder, there was no response. One of her daughters was taking care of her. Jacob found the whole scene most unsettling. How could things have changed so drastically? Till just recently she'd been so vibrant, so alive, so eager to help Jacob sort things out; happily baking cookies for her grandchildren, feeding her chickens, whatever.

A week later, she was gone.

71

Chapter Four

———✿✿✿———

Into The Twenties

*T*hose early twenties were good years, very good years; no doubt the best that Manitoban farmers had ever seen. The rains came at the right time and the crops did well, the prices were high and it looked like that's how they'd stay, nothing got wiped out by grasshoppers or hailstorms. Even the flu bugs people had struggled with had somehow moved on. After the terrible flu in '18, that was something in itself. There was no more talk of war either; no, as pacifists, they had not gotten involved, yet they'd heard the wretched stories. Those were unsettling and everyone had breathed a big sigh of relief when the World War had officially ended. Hopefully, people had learned their lessons and such a tragedy would never occur again.

The Blumenort farmers - the aggressive, hard working, forward looking ones that is, and that entailed about a dozen or more families - were excited about the favourable times. And they cashed in on it wholeheartedly. They built bigger barns and then houses, too; they invested in newer machinery, larger herds, better horses. They planted bigger fields and bought more land. Even though their excellent cash crops paid for much of this, some of them, including Jacob's father, set their sights even higher. They went to the bank for loans to acquire still more land and so were able to buy out the families that were moving to the States to find milder winters as well as some of the less aggressive neighbours and smaller acreages bordering their farms. Soon, the size of their community had expanded significantly.

Jacob's father bought a very expensive stallion during this time. He had always liked working with horses. Now, he had a way of making it more than a hobby – it became a lucrative business. He offered breeding and training services and became well known for both. But it didn't stay there. Due to the skill he had developed, and his natural love of horses and other animals, too, he got to be called upon as a vet on numerous occasions. Although he had never had any official training for it, through the need in the community and the care he could provide, he became a very busy and much appreciated man in the area for a number of years.

It was a heady time for many other people, too - an exhilarating time. Finally, the promise made by their fathers and Grandpas some fifty years ago when they emigrated from Russia, so eager and optimistic, was coming true. These families had reached their own land of *milk and honey*.

And they even remembered, to a fair extent at least, to give thanks.

* * *

Change – constant change was in the air, too. Things were happening.

At the ripe old age of 23 and after only the briefest courting time, brother Peter had, in 1920, married his sweetheart Maria. She, a beautiful young woman, was two years his senior and a member of the Unger clan that resided in the area near Steinbach. They made an attractive couple and Jacob began to dream of emulating that. There was a fine young woman *he* had in mind. If only she would agree.

Could he dare hope for that?

Could he even dare imagine himself having the courage to ask her and find out?

Ach, he wasn't ready to go there. Not yet. He didn't even want to think about it too much. Brooding on his fears would get him nowhere. Instead, he was going to do the right thing and join the church. That way he'd be ready whenever he'd gather up his courage to try.

Going to Instruction Class consisted largely of learning the meaning of the Catechism questions he had already memorized in school. Jacob found this comparatively easy and was frequently able to answer the questions that the ministers asked which in turn made them like him. And the fact that they appreciated him made him strive even harder to please and to aim high for perfection. Was that not, after all, what Christianity was all about?

The very first question in the book boggled his mind and kept him awake at night a few times.

"What is the most important thing a person should strive for in this world?"

"To live in fellowship with God, under His grace, and to inherit eternal life."

No matter how he twirled that around in his mind or how hard he strove for perfection, he just couldn't get to the point where he was sure. Was what he was doing good enough or was he missing something? Should a person even hope to be sure? That catechism answer made it sound as if it had nothing to do with works, and yet the preaching in church usually sounded as if it did. The whole thing was confusing, but he must not - no he dare not - expose his ignorance. Memories of his childhood hurts were still too raw – he couldn't afford to ask for possible frowns of disapproval, so he decided to silently pray instead. Surely, eventually, it would all become clear, wouldn't it?

Of the baptism itself, which took place in Steinbach on Pentecost Sunday, about all he could remember later was that he together with the two church pews full of other young adults – women on one side, men on the other - had simultaneously answered all the seven questions posed them. He never could recall the details; only that he had said he was repenting of his sins (which hopefully weren't that many), and he'd always seek to obey both God and the church (which amounted to about the same thing, right?). He had no intention of ever back-trekking on any of that, so he should be okay. *Surely he should be*, he reasoned.

*   *   *

At his parents' house, some things remained the same. At first. Papi's optimism and aggressive farming for one thing and his gifted leadership in the community. These were constants - it looked like they might never change.

And yet, on June 1ˢᵗ of 1921, the unthinkable happened. While that did not necessarily change the above – at least not immediately - it *was* the hardest imaginable curve, enough to throw his life right upside down.

"Papi, come quick. Come quick. Something is happening to Mami," nine-year old Frank was screaming, panic stricken. Frank did not panic easily. Papi actually dropped the reins of the horse he was training – such an almost daily thing to him - and hollered to whoever could hear him, "Take him and put him away." Jacob was not at home, but Abraham and 15 year old John were nearby and quickly tethered the horse before following Papi to the house.

Papi was kneeling beside Mami on the floor. She had fallen while trying to get into bed.

He was tugging at her, lifting her gently, helping her all the way into the bed. She was not responding. He pleaded with her to wake up, to listen to him, to open her eyes at least one more time. There was nothing.

After several frantic minutes and then several this-can't-be-true minutes, reality slowly seeped in. Papi stumbled to his feet and plunked himself into the nearest chair. His face was ashen and his voice creaked strangely when he asked, "What happened?"

Frank and 10 year-old David stood motionless, wide-eyed and horror struck. The only other witness was 14 year-old Anna. She sounded frightened yet almost calm-like as she whispered, "Mami was sitting in the kitchen. She was tired. We'd been pulling weeds in the garden, you know? And she said we could make some fresh lemonade maybe. We still had two lemons left. But then suddenly she said, 'No Anna, wait.' And she was holding her chest. I think it was hurting her. Then she said 'I'm not feeling good. I will need to lie down.' And she went but she didn't make it. I tried to help her but she was too heavy. . ."

So, he and Anna had been kneeling side by side trying to revive her Mami. In the crisis, Papi had not even realized.

That afternoon, his wife Katharina died very suddenly without warning. Sure, there had been symptoms. Enough for Papi to take her to the doctor, twice actually, to check out the frequent heavy feeling in her chest coupled many times with breathing issues. She would breathe hard and say something like, "Someday, I will run out of air." The doctor had diagnosed her as having a heart condition, but he didn't sound at all alarmed. The spells never lasted very long and she'd seem to be okay again, so no one knew they had reason to worry.

Until now. Now, when it was too late.

*   *   *

There was hardly a dry eye in the service; even more so at the graveyard when all eight of the children participated physically, with shovels, at the burial. It was a warm, sunny day and as even the youngest, 9 ½ year old Frank and almost 11 year-old David, helped energetically; panting, shirt tails flying, sweat mingling with the tears, it was impossible to observe without also being deeply moved.

*   *   *

For Papi, it was déjà vu. He'd been there before, 21 years ago. Yet the details were so vastly different. That had been in the cold of winter. He'd had three babies too small to remember. (Correct that – Peter did have some vague memories it seemed; perhaps just from the retelling. Back in those early years, he had hung out constantly with Papi, like inseparably, and the two had chatted a lot.) And then, too, with Margaret, he had fought the idea, hard; he'd been young and passionately in love, yet he had seen the handwriting on the wall. She had told him herself, and although he hated the very thought, he *knew*. And he remembered how, when they had first talked about it, they had agreed to pray about it together, how they had felt led to ask for one more year and how that was exactly what had been granted them.

Now? Who would ever have guessed that sturdy Katherina, who had borne him five more healthy children and did a good job of raising them and running the household, would suddenly, at the age of 44, collapse of heart disease?

His approach to the grieving process showed perhaps the biggest change. And it must be due to more than just the difference in his age. *Then*, although his heart was utterly crushed and broken, he had forced himself within a shockingly short time to move on; not so much for his own sake – if he'd focused only on himself, he might never have remarried - but his three little sons needed a mother. And it had all worked out – not perfectly, of course, but surprisingly well.

Now, he would take his time. Time to think, to pray, to wait and see. There was no telling what would fall across his path or what God might have in store for him.

In the meantime, the household, although drastically altered, went on. Everyone missed Mami. That was a given and it took a while to adjust. But almost as if on autopilot, the girls took over. Tina, who'd been helping at a neighbour's house, moved back home. She turned nineteen two weeks after the funeral. Although she'd never been known to be particularly strong, aggressive, or brave, she now, slowly but surely, took charge. She did a good job, too, showing more inner strength than had been noticeable before. And Anna, 14, was her sidekick. Between the two, they ran an amazingly efficient household.

*   *   *

For Jacob, it was the beginning of the end of family life as he had known it.

Ever since he was old enough to decide a few things for himself, he had known that, although he'd always been involved on the family farm, he did not find it satisfying. His hankering for carpentry, for building houses and barns and furniture and whatnot, was strong and growing. With Papi's encouragement, he'd gotten his first building job lined up with one of the Plett brothers. He liked it. Pretty soon, he had more.

He'd always be a farmer in one way or another. It was the way of his people. When it came to threshing time, he was part of the crew. When Papi needed something done, he could count on Jacob to help out, be it seeding time or plowing or whatever. But as soon as Jacob could get away, off he'd go to his next building project. That's where he found his biggest joy.

*   *   *

Jacob's personal world came crashing down one lovely summer day a year later when he discovered that the girl he had had his heart set on, the one he had secretly hoped to marry, was betrothed to another. To one of his closest friends, in fact. And he had never even gathered the courage to ask her out.

Now, he would never know. Could it have worked out if he'd been more confident?

And what about his friend? Could it be that he never guessed Jacob's secret intent? Or did he do it on purpose, perhaps even in spite? Talking things out did not come easy to either of them, so they simply didn't.

It took Jacob a long time to overcome the bitter bile that collected in his mouth every time he merely thought about the hurt. And when that finally settled some, discouragement took its place.

Could there be anyone out there that would be right for him? Likely not.

Guess I'll be single for the rest of my life.

*   *   *

It was 1923. Brother Peter and his lovely wife Maria had two children by now, cute little 2 year old Margaret who'd been Papi's only grandchild at the time of Mami's passing, and who was named after her original grandma, and busy little one year old John. They surprised Jacob by inviting him to move in with them.

Really? Jacob hesitated.

"It will be good for you," Peter argued. "It will help you feel more like an adult. More free. Here, you can come and go as you please."

Seeing he wasn't quite convinced yet, Maria piped up, "And you could help with the children every so often. And maybe earn your keep by building things for us. I could even sew some pants for you if you liked."

"But wouldn't I be in the way?"

"No, not at all. We'd love to have you."

He decided to accept the offer. They had a room up in the loft of the house that suited him quite well. And he had so few things of his own, moving in was no big deal.

As it turned out, this was a viable option for all of them. He became like part of the family and loved it. If he couldn't have his own, he could at least enjoy theirs.

And that's how it would remain, through their next six babies and all the ups and downs that go with the raising of a growing family, *for thirteen years.*

*   *   *

Peter and Maria lived about a mile and a half northerly of their parents' farm, toward Greenland, in a set of old buildings. Their home was a weather-beaten long structure built the old way; a house at one end, the barn at the other, and a connecting shelter between the two. This middle part became a sort of all purpose room, and Maria suggested that Jacob could use that space to build things.

He did not need to be coaxed or asked twice. He soon latched on to that space and loved it. Before long, he had built numerous things, developing that as a hobby; children's beds, a few dressers, the odd small table. Then, he decided it was time to create something for himself, and he built the best dresser yet. Maria and the children watched from time to time as he outdid himself, sanding, fine-tuning every corner, and then painting it a shiny yellow. It was lovely and he kept it that way for years. If ever a child would inadvertently leave fingerprints on it, he'd notice, get out his dusting rag, and shine it up all over again. It was one of the first, of the very few things, he had ever called his own and he truly cherished it.

Another thing he cherished was the bicycle he bought to go to work with. Not only did he pick the best quality bike when he purchased it, he also kept it in A1 condition: clean, oiled, and in shape. And neither his brothers nor his nephews would easily get permission to ride it.

But going to work was the big thing in his life. Work was important and he worked hard. Doing a good job was super important, and he always tried to ace whatever he had seen done so far. Second best was never an option. Style and fashion was not on that list, but quality workmanship definitely was, and everyone who knew him quickly knew that about him, too. There were no two ways about that.

This applied to the various houses and barns and sheds he first helped build; then, in later jobs, became the lead carpenter in. It also applied to his job that he kept with the Plett Brothers of PlattiHoff*, part of Blumenort. These businessmen were his friends and co-workers. The company accomplished many things. They made logs, and then they'd plane the wood. They manufactured the big round cheese boxes (cheese making was such an important part of life at the time) together with their perfectly fitted overhanging lids. They built wooden egg crates and created newfangled door hinges, barn door latches, and trap door paraphernalia. Jacob took pride in all these things, and more, but in nothing as much as in their actual building program. In this, he excelled, usually working together with one or the other of the Plett brothers. Sometimes, one of his own brothers would come to help, too.

Chapter Five

———∾∾∾———

More of the twenties and early thirties

A new phenomena had been coming to various communities, including Blumenort and Steinbach and many
others, for some time now. It all began with the news that came
from Russia, from the distant relatives still living there, where
tragedy upon tragedy was happening.

In 1875, when Jacob's grandparents had immigrated to
Canada, many of their people had chosen not to move. Generally
speaking, the ones that decided to stay behind were the ones
that were more affluent, more educated, perhaps more forward
thinking or even more sophisticated. Life was going well for
them, and they saw no reason to re-locate. Nor did they have
any desire to lose their prestige only to adopt the certain-to-be-
poverty-stricken stance of the sojourning pioneer.

But that was then, and now was now. Fate had done its
upside down twist and the tables had been turned. Everything
had changed. At first, there were those, right here in our solid
Christian communities, even in leadership, who took a rather
cold attitude when they heard about the distant sufferings.
*Those people should have come when our families did. Why
didn't they get out when they could, before all the horrors started
happening?*

But the stories coming over only got worse. Countless people,
including many of their distant relatives, were being murdered,
tortured, taken to horrible concentration camps. Survivors, children of well-to-do parents, escaped with only the clothes on
their back and were forced to remain in hiding. Some saw hor-

rendous deeds done to their loved ones, the stuff of nightmares for years to come.

Quite suddenly, there had sprung up a new attitude of compassion. *Our distant, distant cousins need our help*, people started saying. Not everybody agreed or even appreciated this, but in each community, there were those that cared and worked hard at this newly birthed mission. They collected and sent money for basic food and clothes. Then toward the travelling of some lonely escapee. Pretty soon, whole families, what was left of them - many were new widows with children, others were newly made orphans pretending to be part of someone's family - were being sponsored and brought over to safety. This, of course, was not easy. It entailed a lot of paperwork, some smuggling, and lots of delays and complications for one reason or another. And, of course, generous people willing to send the money and pay the bills. But more and more folks were coming through. It was working.

Papi was one of the forward thinking people who was willing to put his money where his mouth was. He had voted *for* it, and he meant that. His stance was very daring; some of his neighbours were totally shocked. It was a first in Blumenort. As a widower, he decided to sponsor a family to come over, and surprisingly, it worked with less hassle than expected. Some of the children in the family had to stay behind (delayed but got through later) for minor issues – one had sore eyes. The new immigrants had to be *very* healthy, the government officials said.

The long and short of that story produced a fairytale ending. The family he sponsored turned out to be a comparatively new widow created by tragedy; someone he had never met or heard of before. But she, Susanna, and Papi ended up falling in love with each other and getting married quite quickly. That happened on February the 17th in 1924, and they lived together happily until death did them part.

Both of them were in their third marriage. Both had families from before but were beyond the childbearing years now. Together, they enjoyed their accumulated large family, accepting each and every one of the children, all sides combined.

Jacob had a hard time digesting all this at first. Some of his brothers were shocked, too; it had happened so fast. The children still living at home were happy, though; they quickly learned to love their new mother. Two and a half years of living without one was long enough; they were very ready.

Eventually, everyone adjusted, and everyone loved their new mother and grandmother. It just took Jacob a little longer.

* * *

Sometimes, in the evenings, Jacob and Peter would sit down on the bench in front of their house just to talk. After a while, a pattern emerged. Both had their passions and could stick up for them dogmatically. Although they loved each other fervently and agreed on many things, when it came to religious stuff - their frequent and favourite topic - they were miles apart. Or so it seemed. And their discussion could become quite heated.

Peter had made tremendous progress spiritually speaking since he became an adult. He said, "It's not by works, Jacob. It's by grace we are saved!" That very thought excited him, and the desire to spread that insight on to others was growing in him. He wanted the church to express that better, the young people in the church to learn it; he wanted to reach out and possibly help some lost neighbour latch on to this grace, too, and what was perhaps most controversial – he didn't care that he was labelled newfangled. At times, that might just be required he argued, letting go of some of the old ways to make room for the new.

"But," Jacob sputtered, "even if there is truth in all that, I can't think of a better way to serve God than by being faithful to the church. Rebellion is not godly nor is it right to constantly rock the boat. Our leaders knew what they were doing when they made the rules, so instead of trying to change things, why don't we just simply obey?"

Yes, why indeed?

That discussion went on for years without coming to a good consensus. It was as if they were each looking at a coin from one side only, and neither side made it complete.

But how easy is that to admit?

* * *

Life - both the circumstances (like the things that happened in his childhood) and the choices he had made in response - had made Jacob into who he was. That had led him to become both a conservative person and a perfectionist. This combination made him come across as stern and unyielding, frequently wearing a frown as he concentrated on getting something just right and sounding judgemental when someone did something that didn't feel right to him. Some of the children in the community, such as the youngsters at PlattiHoff, found this unsettling, just a tad scary, and so they tended to shy away from him.

The children that knew him best though saw his other side. He loved them. Peter and Maria's children, one after the other, became great and loyal friends of his, and the relationships that developed became a constant that he cherished for the rest of his life.

* * *

Although Jacob lived with Peter and Maria and not with his father and stepmother, he visited often enough to keep a close tab on things. Changes kept happening at his parents' home; too fast, sometimes. The younger siblings were growing up rapidly; the older ones getting married or at least planning to. He didn't quite know how to feel about that; everyone seeming to get ahead faster than he did, but he didn't try to stop them. Outwardly at least, he was stoic and strong, and he wished them all well. If his turn would come up eventually, good and fine; if not, so be it.

Abraham's story took everyone by surprise at first, even Maria who had said vehemently that such a thing would never happen. But then, how could she have known?

When the good news arrived, it was not totally unexpected and yet, in a way, it was. Stepmother Susanna's daughter Margaret, aged 20, had been held back in the emigration process, encountering many delays. Now, no doubt in answer to fervent prayers, she had been cleared and was on her way. She would need to be picked up at the train station.

Papi and Susanna decided that asking Abraham to do this errand would be the logical choice. He was not immediately convinced. "No way," he said. "I am too shy." Besides, since none of the family had yet met Margaret, he had only Susanna's description to go by. How would that work, trying to connect with a total stranger in public among all those people? Could he even expect to recognize her?

Somehow, he let himself be persuaded. But as he went, some of his reluctance gave way to his adventure-loving spirit which was part of who he was.

Margaret, on the other hand, when she finally reached Manitoba, dead tired from the long journey, was getting more and more excited about meeting her new family. She had no idea who was coming for her, of course, but she had the letters from Mother. Apparently, and this was still hard to grasp – could it actually be true - Mother was happily married, since February to a wonderful man whom Margaret had never met, but in that process, she had inherited eight new siblings. Wow! Maybe one of her new brothers would come to get her from the station.

*   *   *

Margaret and Abraham were intrigued with each other from the very start; yes, they felt shy and awkward for a little while in the beginning, although they'd had no trouble finding each other, but a bond began happening that would last forever.

First though, there were obstacles to overcome. One immediate one was that Margaret was pretty well forced to go to work on the West reserve for the family that had helped pay her extra bills for travelling and all that was involved. That was just the way it went, and it seemed fair enough. If someone sponsored you, they could expect, once you got here, you'd voluntarily go work for them to pay them back for their efforts.

The second one was an inner kind of tug-of-war for Abraham. The way he'd been raised and the way a lot of people in the community talked, this new relationship was a scary thing. "The young people that come from Russia are not our kind. They have a different way of thinking. You should just leave them alone," someone told him adamantly.

"Why so? What makes you say that?"

"Well, they are just different. They worship differently. They pray aloud at the table. They sing new fashioned songs. Their brides wear white. The girls wear necklaces. . ."

The list went on and on, but Abraham got the point. This was something he would have to grapple with. Their church had chosen Romans 12 verses one and two as a focal point and one they really pushed. According to their interpretation of that scripture, most of these differences would be classified as worldly, and one is not supposed to be worldly. So, Abraham had a dilemma, and it was not an easy one to solve.

Till now, he had been loyally conservative, like Jacob and many others in the area. But his attraction to Margaret was strong. And he was, by nature, a bit of a risk taker. Maybe he could make it work. Maybe Margaret would be agreeable, be willing to compromise some and basically obey. Maybe he could have the best of both worlds.

* * *

On a chilly spring day, on April the 8th in 1925, Abraham and Margaret were married.

He was 25, she was 21, and they loved each other dearly.

Yes, every so often through the years those tug-of-war issues that he had been warned about did come up and sometimes even resurfaced again, but they always worked them through. Not only did they survive, they learned to thrive.

* * *

1926 was a most memorable year for Jacob. It was the year he bought his first car, a spanking new Model T with all the latest features, including velvety curtains at the windows. His was the first car among the young people in the community, and it got glamorized a lot. Boys would hang around the car often, like after church or even in town, just to ogle it. He loved the attention – for a while, at least. There was nothing conservative about his approach to that car. He had bought the best, as far as he could tell, and kept it tuned and spotless in as much as he was able, dirt roads notwithstanding.

Yet once the newness wore off, he was still lonely. The attention did not fill that empty spot in his heart. Nor did it help seeing Peter's strong marriage blossom and produce more lovely children, all of whom he loved.

Now, if only there was a chance he could emulate that!

* * *

On a hot summer day, on July the 25th, 1926, Jacob's brother John married Helena Barkman.

Then, on June 30th of 1928, sister Tina married Cornelius Reimer. Then, his brother David started courting his stepmother's grand-daughter Helen Braun.

Jacob tried to be happy for them, but he felt the sting of it, too. Long since, he had seen every single girl he'd ever had even the slightest crush on walk the aisle with someone else. Feelings of discouragement threatened him. No matter how much he strived for perfection, his overwhelming conclusion remained in place. He simply wasn't good enough.

Then, before David got to marry Helen, his intended, the tables got turned, *again*. This time, it was Papi who got ill. After a mere three week struggle with stomach cancer, he succumbed to it on October the first, 1931. He was 60 years old, Susanna two years older. His youngest child, Frank, was almost twenty.

Now, if the whole truth be told, Papi's troubles had begun much earlier.

He had many good things going for him, of course. He was happily married. He and Susanna had quite recently made the trip of their lifetime, in Jacob's car, to the west coast, enjoying everything that entailed.

He had owned his own car, a basic Model T, for a number of years already. He liked that car (although for that trip, he'd wanted to use Jacob's nicer one), and he liked the feeling of control it gave him when he drove it. Feeling in charge of a situation had always satisfied him; it was part and parcel of who he was. Every time that feeling had been taken from him, even temporarily, he'd been crushed. But being the go-getter that he was, he never stayed down long. He could rise to almost any situation. Obviously, God had gifted him for leadership, in the family, in church matters, in the community, in various aspects of farming and finances, too. But the latter is where the heart-break came in.

Without warning, dry years had sprung on them, one after the other, and he wasn't yet finished paying off the loans he had made so optimistically, so aggressively. He had wanted each of his children to inherit at least a small farm for starters. Suddenly, the crops were poor, the prices were low, and the banks were putting on pressure. Like it or not, the dirty thirties had come, and he was not ready. What should he do? What could he do?

If stress is related to getting cancer, who knows if that is what did him in?

In the end, his sons had to help finish up what he left unfinished. They were able to save most of the land and properties, barely, but not all. And Jacob for one vowed that he would never make that kind of mistake; not if he could help it. The pain was not worth it.

* * *

Every so often, Jacob liked to get together with his cousin Jacob.

They had a lot of things in common. The name, of course, but there was more. Their parents were siblings from both sides, so the two were double first cousins and shared every single relative equally. Jacob had fond memories of looking up to his namesake cousin who was a few years older than he. As children, they used to get together often. The downside of that was that his cousin knew his every foible, every mistake he'd ever made. But maybe that was also good. At least they understood each other and never needed to put up a front.

As they grew up, their paths had become more separated; not totally, but more so. His cousin chose to marry young, and before long, he and Maria had a large and growing family. That put the two in very different situations. His cousin also struggled some but with different issues. He tried to farm but had a hard time developing that; he tried other work but had a harder time figuring out where he fit. It seemed for awhile that the older Jacob was a wee bit jealous of the younger, but that didn't last forever. Once he too was able to afford a car, even though it was not a luxury model, that problem never surfaced again.

It was on a Sunday afternoon that Jacob decided to stop in at the Friesens – his cousin's place. He had a great big thought nibbling at his mind and he needed help. His cousin's wife Maria had an unmarried sister who was taking care of her widowed mother in Kleefeld. Her name – Tina - was on his mind a lot lately. He'd like to find out if she'd be interested in a relationship with him, but he was scared stiff, way too shy to ask her.

"Would you . . . would you be able to ask her for me? Sort of feel your way and find out if there's a chance." he asked his cousin very carefully.

"Sure," Jacob was more than willing.

And he kept his word. He sent Maria.

* * *

When the news came back a few weeks later that Tina was not interested, at least not for now, he was disappointed. Part of him felt crushed and yet there was a tiny window of hope. Maybe. . . maybe some day?

He didn't have other options he wanted to pursue. On his down days, he felt depressed, but on his good days, which were coming much more often now, he prayed about it. If God were in it – well, you just never know.

* * *

Almost a year to the date later, cousin Jacob found him at his worksite, busily building.

The clatter of the car and the unexpected visit was a welcome intrusion on this strangely warm and sweaty kind of early fall day. He had a letter for Jacob.

Surprised, Jacob perused it carefully, then stuck it in his overall pocket. As soon as his cousin was gone – he had stayed to chat for only a few minutes - Jacob put down his hammer and found a spot behind the barn, away, hopefully, from any curious eyes. He sat down on the stump there and with shaking fingers carefully opened the letter.

That letter made his day.

It did much more, too. It turned his life around.

That letter was the first step toward forever changing him. And once the shock of it settled down a bit, he spent the rest of the afternoon whistling his favourite praise song, *Groszer Gott wir Loben Dich.**

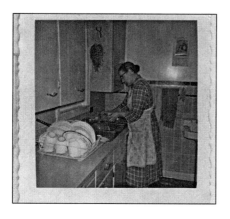

Tina, happily washing dishes in her
modern kitchen

Jacob's father, Peter I. Wiebe, with
his third wife, 1930

Jacob and Tina's twin boys,
summer 1938

Jacob and Tina with daughter Frieda,
at her wedding to Vic Loewen. By this
time conservative rules have relaxed a
fair bit. August 1967

Peter and Maria Wiebe, Jacob's brother. This is the couple with whom Jacob lived for thirteen years

Jacob and Tina washing son Alvin's car as a surprise for him.

Jacob and Tina's six children. Picture taken specially for that momentous first trip to Mexico 1952

Jacob and Tina at their large garden plot

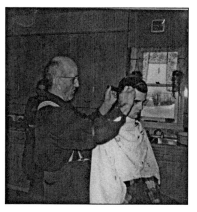

Jacob just finished kneading
bread dough in that large silver bowl

Jacob, giving son Jim a haircut

Jacob and Tina, pleased to pose with
their first grandchildren

The five sets of twins, all boys, all Wiebes, all first cousins. This
picture appeared in the Carillon News 1950-51.

AND NEVER

THE TWAIN

SHOULD

MEET?

———⟨⟩———

Chapter One

---··◌◌◌··---

1936 – 1938

 *J*acob worked faster than usual to finish the beautiful cherry wood writing desk he was making for himself; it had all the latest features – curved lines, rolled top, doors at the top, drawers toward the bottom, nice dark shellac finish, shiny brass pulls. *Who knows? I may just be creating my own wedding gift.*

*　*　*

By this time, Jacob was long since into his second car – another beauty. A 1930 Model. A Ford; a 4-door Sedan. No, it wasn't new at the moment, but when Jacob was done shining it up, he could have fooled anyone. It sure looked brand new. And for that Sunday, he had every reason to polish it extra well.

Tina, too, was prepared. The house was clean. She was wearing her newest dress – the one she made for and had just worn to her brother's wedding. She had baked her best cookies, the soft molasses. What more could she do?

*　*　*

October the 4th. The date would be forever ingrained in their brains. Yet some of those details got lost in the shuffle, dissolved in a blur that could never be clearly recalled again. For one thing, it was Tina's brother Bernhard's wedding day. She had expected it to feel tumultuous, and it did, but not in the way she had anticipated. Bernhard and Anna were married, in Steinbach thankfully, so Tina didn't have to be involved with the hosting, just the helping. But instead of dwelling on the pain of seeing him marry and leave her behind, she had other pressing thoughts to fill her mind. The immediacy of those, and the feeling of urgency that seemed to come along with them, overruled everything else and created for awhile a blurry cloud that threatened to engulf her.

That didn't last though. Hadn't she been learning to trust God in all circumstances?

She never could explain what happened that night. Not really. Not the details, at least.

Was it love at first sight? Ah, second sight might be more accurate, but the symptoms could look the same, couldn't they?

Or were they just so very ready? Desperate to lose their lonely singleness perhaps or maybe just so willing to run with this new opportunity before them?

Or so sure that this was what God wanted?

Whatever it was, run with it they did. There was no hesitation. They had prayed and God appeared to be leading. They set the date – November the 1st.

That left them only weeks to get ready. Busy, busy weeks. Jacob secured them a place to live on the PlattiHoff* in Blumenort. It was generously offered to him as part of his job benefits – a smallish, older house that no one was living in at the moment. It required a good scrubbing but was pretty weather proof – it should be okay for starters. Jacob also hustled up the furniture, between his own and the hand-me-downs he picked up from his brothers. They didn't need much, did they? And he was already dreaming of the tall chest of drawers he would build Tina next winter. It would be dark and . . . perfect. And their own table that he'd build . . . maybe the following year. . . .hmm. . .

Tina sewed a dress for herself. Brown dresses were in vogue at the time in her circles, and she made sure it was the nicest cloth she could find, and she sewed it well. Then, she began on the aprons. It was fashionable at the time to have pretty little aprons offered to all the girls who would serve food. Tina chose white ones with pink ruffles and had fun making them. They turned out really well, too; nice and pretty.

Preparing the food was the next adventure; for this, of course, she had a lot of help from both sides of the family. Wedding feasts were always a joint communal type effort.

She and Jacob, in his nice new looking car, went around the community and among the relatives, announcing their intentions and inviting everybody to the wedding. She thought at first she'd find that intimidating, and Jacob had struggled with a similar fear for himself.

"But this is what has to be done, so we'll just do it. Right?" Jacob said. It worked, and with every person they told, their own excitement grew.

On the 24th, they had their Filafnis*, which they held at Tina's mother's little house. A lot of relatives and friends came, the food was good, a feeling of joy and excitement floated in the air despite the cold north wind that was blowing and giving everyone occasional shivers.

On the wedding day, the weather was balmy, blowing gentle breezes only. Tina hoped that was a sign of smooth sailing ahead. The service was held in Blumenort, much like every other morning service, except for the two chairs up front, centre aisle. Rev. David P. Reimer, a favourite minister of both of them, preached, and when he was done, he announced their intentions and called Jacob and Tina forward. Nervously, they proceeded but afterwards couldn't even recall how the questions had gone; only that they solemnly said their "I do's."

* * *

The reception was held at Jacob's parents' old place, in the big shed. A temporary wood stove was set up for heat, tables were made of long boards laid on saw horses, and the serving girls were beautiful in their fancy aprons. And the food was terrific; everybody outdid themselves. The stacks of cookies Tina had managed to make were a real hit and begun a new saying among her newly made relatives – *if you want good cookies, ask Tina. She's the best cookie baker yet.*

There were gifts, too. A new cooking pot, some dishes and tableware, two baking pans, some little things that would come in handy in the kitchen, a couple of towels. Each was appreciated.

*   *   *

Moving to PlattiHoff* proved to be both interesting and challenging for Tina. It was a close, tightly-packed neighbourhood of about half a dozen families, all knowing each other well. Not only did they live close together, they were all family - brothers, cousins, nephews; everyone except Jacob and Tina. Even Jacob felt like he could be related – he had worked there so long and got along well with all of them.

But Tina was definitely the *immigrant,* and she felt it.

In her lonely moments, she phoned Ma; she sorely missed her. She was thankful for how things had worked out though. Bernhard and Anna had moved in with Ma when Tina had married so she had never been left alone. Now, when she called their house, she could talk with any of the three, and she liked that. Jacob had made it one of his first priorities to see that Ma had a good working telephone in her house and Tina, too, of course.

Jacob was good to Tina - in so many ways. On many Sundays, they went to visit Ma and sometimes her siblings. Other Sundays, it was his siblings they'd visit. Always they went happily; Jacob was obviously pleased to show off his new wife. And he honoured her relatives as well as his own. He was pleased with her cooking and with her housekeeping skills. When he realized that she could drive a car, he encouraged her to drive theirs all by herself to go visit family occasionally, especially when she had news to share or had things on her heart. That kind of trust really made her day.

And there really *was* big news. Her longings would be fulfilled, her loneliness largely solved, she was quite certain, come September. She had always looked forward to having a family – *as long as I don't have too many babies too soon . . . one per year I think I could handle.*

100

* * *

Jacob's work that winter had a few unexpected adventures thrown in, just to make life interesting no doubt.

They were building sleighs; various kinds, with all the needed accessories, including the popular canvas covered styles called the Kabitt Schlayde.*

Jacob and Peter Plett had just finished building one of those, a nice sturdy canvas covered sleigh for a family in the Morris area. Usually, a client would come for the finished product with his team of horses and take the sleigh home the traditional way. This time was an exception. The customer called and asked them to hand deliver the sleigh and as soon as possible – he *really* needed it. He even offered to pay a little extra for the courtesy.

This was a first for the two, and they brainstormed as to how they would do it. Although they owned horses and used them regularly, neither of the men were ardent horse lovers like Jacob's Pa had been and dreaded the very thought of making the couple of days' journey the normal way. There had to be an alternative. There had to be.

Which of them thought of it first no one ever discovered. Perhaps the idea had sprung on them simultaneously. Instead of drawing the sleigh with horses, they would pull it with Jacob's car, securing the Diestel* snugly to the back bumper of the Model A. Since there was still a lot of snow around, the driving might be a bit of a challenge, but they were ready to give it a try. Taking along a few shovels and ropes and stuff, and extra food, of course, they set out despite the trepidation of concerned wives.

Neighbours were watching. Mothers called children to come and see – soon, there were rows of faces plastered against the rapidly steaming up windows in the various houses. Some moved outside to get a closer view. One of the young boys said much later, "That was the funniest memory of my childhood. How I wish some one had had a camera – a good movie camera."

The sleigh was attached securely, but it seemed to have a mind of its own. It bounced up and down like crazy - too light to travel empty. Horse drawn sleighs always have at least one person in them, but the men had not considered that angle. Soon, they figured out the perfect solution. One of them would sit in the sleigh while the other drove. And they'd trade off every so often to get warmed up. It worked.

Neighbours' laughter notwithstanding, and bravely, successfully overcoming every snowy unplowed stretch on the road, they got there all in good condition in one day. Yes, after their arrival, they did have to bed down for the night, but only for one night. Had they done it with horses, it would likely have involved three or four.

*   *   *

"You will need to have a doctor and be planning to go to the hospital to have the baby," the midwife told Tina, early mid-summer.

"Really? Why?"

"I am not sure, but something seems different than the usual. I want you double checked by someone who knows."

When Tina told Jacob, he didn't hold back. *Definitely* they would go to the doctor and check things out. Flashbacks of childhood memories and stories flooded his brain. He recalled hearing Mami say, "When a woman is pregnant, she has one foot in the grave."

The very thought gave him goose bumps.

The doctor confirmed what the midwife had said and more. He also, sort of, put their minds at ease. When the right day came, they definitely would be going to the hospital; the doctor predicted that it would be earlier than anticipated. He also told them a secret – which, of course, they told no one.

*   *   *

August 22nd. *It is time.* Tina knew it. *Am I ready for this? Can I do this, and times two? We're married less than 10 months, and I thought one baby a year would be more than enough.*

August 23rd. The hospital was doing a great job and so was Tina. The twins arrived in good shape – or so the doctor said. Two screaming little boys. Wow!

Jacob was allowed to see mother and little ones after all the clean up was done. Jacob smiled broadly, almost giddy-like, strangely wanting to laugh and cry at the same time, pleased and proud but trembling at the knees and almost everywhere else, too. *Why would a grown man struggle with tears at a moment like this – perhaps one of the happiest of his life? And feel winded like he could have run for miles?*

* * *

The twins were a major novelty. Everybody *had* to see them. Nobody at PlattiHoff had twins and nobody among the relatives either. It was very special.

There was some teasing of course. "You're making up for lost time, eh?' Jacob heard numerous times.

They named them Bernhard and Gerhard, which would eventually get shortened to Ben and George. They were identical, so this created a lot of fun moments. Tina was the only one who could *always* tell them apart. Very soon, both Jacob and the maid he had hired got the hang of it, too. But everyone else kept trying and seldom got it right.

"How do you do it?" several admirers had asked, but Tina only smiled. *Don't mothers just know such things?*

Tina's nightmare with them began when she realized that they weren't growing as well as other babies did. Was her milk not good? She started supplementing with cow's milk, but it made no difference. People were starting to talk – behind her back - wondering if she was somehow an incompetent mother. She felt so small, so frustrated; what was wrong? She had always helped with her many nieces and nephews and never encountered this. Why now? Why were her babies weaker and slower to develop than everyone else's?

At first, Jacob had attributed the problem to nerves; he had heard that new mothers often struggled with similar challenges whether there was reason or not, so he simply tried to be patient and helpful. Once Jacob saw the depth of her concern, though, he quickly agreed to take them back to the doctor for a check-up.

The doctor agreed that they had a problem and diagnosed them both with a form of rickets. "Nothing that can't be fixed though," he said cheerfully and gave them two kinds of drops: tonic water and vitamins. He further gave them advice about healthy eating and mentioned that the tendency toward this condition often ran in families. That thought slapped Jacob hard as he recalled the story of his own childhood. *Could this really be happening to him?*

The doctor remained optimistic through more visits and more drops, and it turned out he was right. By the time the boys had their first birthday, they were almost as strong and healthy as any other child; shortly after that, the problem disappeared entirely and never surfaced again. Both Jacob and Tina thanked God for this answer to their prayers.

*   *   *

One sultry end-of-August day when the boys had just turned one, and Tina was already showing child number three that was on its way, she had the scare of her lifetime.

The boys loved the outdoors. They weren't quite walking yet, but they crawled really well and loved to play with blocks or even sticks and stones, anything their busy little fingers could get a hold of. Tina always watched them very closely. Sometimes, though, since they liked it outside so much and since there were always many children around who were eager to help, she'd let someone watch them while she snuck away for a needed little break, maybe going to the washroom or perhaps putting on a pot of potatoes to boil for supper. That's what she was doing this time.

A threshing crew was busy just beyond their big multi family / business yard. The machine was clattering noisily; men were hollering; several teams of horses were pulling in the loads of sheaves from the freshly cut grain fields. At the site, some of the horses pranced restlessly, running short on their patience while waiting for the unloading to get done. It was a hustling bustling kind of day out there, but Tina was only mildly interested. Her own family had never been into the farming scene enough to get very involved with a threshing outfit. A little bit, yes, but mostly observing from a distance, and that's what she did now. Jacob's was different. They were not only involved, they owned their own outfit and that's where Jacob was today – busy, working with his brothers on the family's farms.

Tina hurried as she stoked up the fire and put on the pot of potatoes. She was about to go back to her babies when she heard a most unusual commotion and some horrific screaming coming from the children outside. *What in the world?*

She started running, but before she got very far, she stopped in her tracks. *What was going on here?* All she could see in her horror was the wagonless but still partly harnessed up team of large horses with reins dangling and the broken evener dragging jerkily behind. The clatter of that scared the horses even more, and the more they ran, the worse it got. They were running helter skelter in crazy loops across the yard. The frightened screaming children had somehow managed to find hiding spots, but in their frenzy, no one had thought to pick up the babies. Alone and unattended, they sat in the middle of the yard very close to where Tina had left them safely just moments before. Now, those crazed creatures were heading straight toward them.

Too shocked to move, with mouth hanging open, she watched what seemed like a movie.

Her soul screeched *God,* but no words spilled out. Those horses were going to kill her babies, both of them, and there was nothing she could do to prevent it. They were coming so fast and so wickedly, there was no way out. Then, in one sudden last-second swerve, the horses swung sideways and looped around the babies before continuing their maddening flight eastward.

Trembling, tears beginning to stream down her face, she rushed out to her babies. She just wanted to hug them forever. But they weren't even crying. They seemed to sense that something was wrong, but they were totally unharmed. As she sat there on the ground holding them, the children came out of hiding and clustered around her. Men seemed to be running everywhere now, trying to catch the runaway horses, coming to check on her and the babies. Someone must have told them what was happening. They measured the distance between the closest horse hoof marks and the spot where the babies sat; it was only inches apart.

Tina couldn't stop trembling, and the neighbour ladies sympathized. There were no snide remarks about her, only about those awful horses. No one seemed to know exactly what had spooked them, but everyone was relieved and thankful; by God's divine hand, a terrible tragedy had been averted. One of the women stayed with Tina till Jacob came home and several people told him the story.

"Miracles still happen, and I am so glad," Jacob repeated several times as they were getting ready for bed; the babies already sound asleep. His whispered bedtime prayer sounded louder and more fervent than usual, and Tina echoed her own private amen.

"Yes, thank you Lord for our miracle."

1938

December arrived with fresh bundles of snow drifting up around the house, but inside the little old farmhouse in PlattiHoff, a different bundle arrived. On the 16th, Tina gave birth to their first daughter, Elizabeth, later called Betty, at home, assisted by a midwife, and everything went well.

Both Jacob and Tina were pleased and proud. The boys were blue eyed and blond like Jacob. The new baby was brown eyed and dark haired like Tina, and secretly, she was thrilled. The baby was healthy and content, but even with the maid that Jacob hired for the first couple of months, Tina's plate was very full. *Who would have guessed that she'd have three babies by just after their second anniversary?*

The twins had learned to walk by now and were starting to be quite mischievous. *If one toddler can spell trouble, two don't just double it; they triple it*, Tina often thought. *Perhaps that's because they stimulate each other so much that their ideas (and pranks) simply magnify and mushroom all out of proportion.*

Sometimes, her sisters tried to give her a break by taking one of the boys. That didn't work. Both of them pined so pathetically for each other, it was too heartbreaking. Then, someone came up with an idea that not only promoted quite a few chuckles, it helped solve the problem. *Prop up a good sized mirror at the child's eye level where he can easily see it and find out what happens*. Wow! The child sees himself. For an identical twin, that is powerful. He thinks he's seeing his brother and plays contentedly nearby.

There had been a whole new shift on the scenario that November. On the 9th, Jacob's brother, Peter, and Maria welcomed a set of twin boys, Edward and Alfred, surprising everyone. It was to be their tenth and final baby. Now, they had eleven. Peter actually apologized to Jacob for the earlier teasing he'd done – he seemed to have a fresh burst of respect for his brother.

What neither of the brothers knew, of course, was that they had unwittingly started a trend in the Wiebe family. This would eventually lead them to the status of front page notice in the then current version of the Carillon News. More twins would be born of their other brothers, each set identical twins, all Wiebes, all boys, all flourishing, within a few years of each other until there'd be five sets.

Jacob enjoyed romping with his little sons in his spare time. But never for very long. Sometimes, he found their endless supply of energy daunting and overwhelming. His desire for perfection kicked in, too. Desperately, he wanted to be a *very* good father who would raise *very* good children, but how was that possible when they were such a handful? Some days, he felt frustrated, even irritated, by their constant prattle and trouble making skills. Then, he'd get into the super strict mode; surely that would help. But more and more often, he'd start brooding on what his father had taught him so carefully –*children, especially boys, must be raised on a farm.*

Had Papi been right? Did that rule count even if a man loved the carpentry world much more than farming?

Chapter Two

———∽∾∽———

1940

*1*940 would, for good reasons and bad, be chalked up as one of the most memorable years ever for both Jacob and Tina. Some of these events would be so life changing it would take Tina a long time until she would feel like her normal self again.

One of the biggest was what was happening with Tina's Ma. The relationship between the two had remained strong; the years Tina had been her sole caregiver were forever etched in their hearts, and they got together as frequently as was conveniently possible. Lately, Ma had seemed reflective, though, had even given Tina some extra fervent hugs and she didn't know why. Sure, there had been various health issues over the last years but nothing life-threatening. She was getting older, less agile and less energetic. But she turned sixty-nine on her recent birthday in February. So, that was understandable, wasn't it? Nothing quite explained the unease on Tina's heart.

Perhaps, the feeling had grown on her earlier than Tina had realized. Ma had been living, for the last winter, with her older son Peter and his wife Anna and some of their lovely adopted children (the first daughter had already gotten married a few years before). That had all been going well until Anna got ill and had to be in the hospital, in Winnipeg, for some time. At this point, Bernhard and Anna invited Ma back to their place so she was living with them again - temporarily, Peter had said.

It was the beginning of April. One day, Tina got a phone call from Bernhard. "Everybody at our house is sick, very sick," he said. "Anna and both of the girls. They have a high fever and sore throats, and I don't know what to do with them."

"Are you asking me to come and help you?"

"I don't know. If you were still living here, I would."

He sounded a little lonely and sad and it tugged at her heart. But going there to help was really out of the question unless she could get someone to keep her babies. And Jacob, she knew, was too busy for that.

What should she do?

"Maybe you should take them all to the doctor," Tina finally suggested. Bernhard liked that idea. Sick as they were, he'd bundle them all up and go find out what was wrong and hopefully get some medicine, too.

Her suggestion worked, but her plan to find a way to go out there to help did not. In fact, it boomeranged in her face as her world turned upside down.

*   *   *

Bernhard was trying to take care of his precious ones as best he could, but nothing worked. Yesterday's medicine from the doctor wasn't helping. Both girls (Lorna, 3, and Sara, 1) were getting worse, the breathing harder and horribly raspy; they seemed to be burning up with fever and more unconscious than alive. Anna wasn't as bad but too sick and weak to help, and now Ma had gotten it, too. When he helped her out of the car yesterday, he'd noticed that the whole seat where she sat was hot to the touch. "That's scary," he told Anna. ""She may be the sickest of us yet." And he didn't know what to do. Who could he ask for help? *Perhaps, this thing was even contagious . . .*

His desperate thoughts were interrupted rudely by the rattle of a car on the driveway, and he turned to see who it might be.

Really? His mouth dropped open in surprise. The doctor and some woman he didn't know. And they were getting out of the car as if they had a purpose, businesslike. *What in the world?*

He didn't have to wait long. The doctor had news, and he did not hesitate for a moment to announce it. "Your family has diphtheria. All of them. I thought as much yesterday, but I had to confirm it. Now, I know, the tests proved it. And you're quarantined. You may not leave, and nobody can come and go. Nobody. This is serious business. But I brought you a nurse," he added more gently. "She will help you with the sick ones."

Bernhard stared at the doctor, feeling like an idiot. Was he sleep-walking or was this real? And how was he supposed to react?

The doctor must have sensed his struggle. "Take me to the children first," he said, sounding kinder. Suddenly, the nurse was at his side, ready to help.

"These children are very ill," he said gravely after examining them, looking at Bernhard. "They may not . . . uh . . . we'll see what we can do." And he proceeded to give the nurse instructions.

Bernhard had a hard time breathing. He'd clearly caught the unspoken prediction. *The doctor was not expecting the children to live.* But now, he was examining Ma. When he straightened beside her bed he sighed. "Your mother, too. And that's strange for a person her age. I . . . ur. . .I can promise you nothing. Ah . . . we'll see." He shook his head as if to clear it.

When he'd left his instructions, he went back to the car to get the quarantine papers and his little hammer. "Remember what I said. Nobody leaves and nobody comes here. Is that clear? If we don't nip this in the bud, it could spread like wild fire – everywhere. And yes, there will be a law enforcement officer out to check and make sure everybody's co-operating." He nailed the sign on their front door; another one, on a stake, was strung up on the driveway. There were more on the backseat. Was he going to put those down the road?

*   *   *

The next day, Anna was feeling slightly better – able to sit up in bed, at least. But the other three were worse. How that was possible, Bernhard could not imagine. He tried to be thankful for two things – that he had not gotten sick yet (unless that ache in the pit of his stomach was the beginning) and that he had a very efficient nurse. To make sure they had something to eat, relatives were allowed to drop off food in a box on the road. After they were gone, Bernhard could go and fetch it. That proved to be very helpful. Not that he felt like eating, but both the nurse and he needed to keep up their strength.

*   *   *

The only way to communicate was the telephone. When Tina got that next call, she was aghast. She had not seen Bernhard cry since he was a little boy, but he sure sounded choked up now. She couldn't blame him – poor guy. *What could she do, though?*

It was then that she thought of it, and she told him, "We're going to pray for a miracle, Bernhard. If we ever needed a miracle, it is now, and I know God can do it."

*   *   *

Tina couldn't wait to hear what was happening when she called the next morning. Bernhard sounded more optimistic. "Little Sara woke up with a smile today. The fever is gone, and she's all clear-headed. I think we've had our first miracle."

That was wonderful news.

That is one down, and two more to go.

The next morning it was Lorna. "She is waking up and looking around, quite alert. Her throat and mouth are still very sore; I don't know when she'll start eating, but the fever has broken and there's hope now. She will not die." Bernhard choked up again. The 3-year-old was a very precious daughter, and the doctor had clearly not expected her to live. And for three whole days, it had looked like he'd be right.

That is two down, and one more to go.

But Ma was not getting better. The nurse was in regular contact with the doctor who was the only one coming and going. (Even the milk from the few cows had to be dumped in case it was contaminated)

At the nurse's call of concern, the doctor came back again. He was pleased at the apparent progress of the little girls, something he had not expected. But checking on Ma, he simply shook his head. Barring an unusual miracle, it was only a matter of time. There was nothing he or anyone else could do.

Hours later, the doctor's prediction came true. It was April the 12th. Ma, Mrs. Elizabeth Unger Kornelsen, died of diphtheria, alone in her bed, in Kleefeld, attended by the nurse and her youngest son.

All the family was called, of course, but nobody could come. The quarantine was ongoing and strictly enforced. And that led up to one of the strangest funerals ever. Tina called it *the funeral that wasn't,* and the sting of it hurt so bad she never ever was able to talk about any of the details.

Others did though. Apparently, it was a closed coffin (very unusual at the time) carried by designated pallbearers who were not part of the family; it had to remain outside (could not be in the church building) and be buried by designated adults only. Women and children as well as any other funeral-goers were not allowed to come even near it. Bernhard and Anna could not attend the funeral or the after glow gathering at Peter Kornelsen's house, which at this point, was the original old family homestead.

* * *

After all was said and done, Jacob and Tina decided to do some research of their own. They borrowed a medical book from the church bishop and looked up *diphtheria.* They needed to understand, to know, what it was and why it was so dangerous.

Diphtheria, they found, is an inflammation in the lining of the respiratory tract. If and when it spreads, it involves other organs as well. It is transmitted most often through close contact by airborne respiratory droplets or by direct contact with secretions from infected people and is considered highly contagious. Its basic symptoms are a sore throat, a high fever, hoarseness, and difficulty breathing, swallowing, or both. Severe neck swelling and enlarged neck lymph nodes can develop, which can lead to suffocation and death; it can also lead to cardiac and neurological complications which too can sometimes lead to death.

What they couldn't figure out though was – where does it come from in the first place?

They never got an answer to that. But when, shortly after this, the new invention of doing vaccinations found its way into their part of the country, they latched on to it quickly. Every one of their children, as soon as it was feasible, got vaccinated for diphtheria. And as that new trend became more widespread, the custom of the quarantines soon disappeared entirely.

*   *   *

Traumatic grieving notwithstanding, life went on.

Jacob's conscience had been spurring him forward. He *needed* to move his family to the farm, and his best option, as far as he could tell, was to build a brand new home on the piece of land he had inherited from his parents along the present #311, two miles west of the #12. He and Tina had been discussing it and were in agreement. They sketched up plans and dreamt of the possibilities. For Tina, this would be the closest thing to well-off that she had ever encountered. For Jacob, it would entail a lot of hard work. He would be his own engineer and contractor, plus the hands-on carpenter. For some of the big parts, such as raising walls and roofs, the community style volunteer system would come in handy. He had helped countless others; surely, he could now expect the favour returned.

Jacob had already begun the preparation stage of the work at the time of his mother-in-law's funeral. He took time off, sincerely trying to honour Tina's needs and those of her family. Yet he didn't want to let himself be stalled too much. There were other deadlines to consider, not the least of which was the upcoming baby for the end of July.

He wanted them all to be moved and settled in long before that, but before that could happen, a home site had to be built up from scratch. It may be plain and simple, but there was no time to lose. The doing of it had to be now, starting with the house. The barn could come a little later.

It worked. Should we say rather, they worked, and they worked hard and they succeeded. By the end of June they were ready; various family members came to help, and the move went quite smoothly, babies and all.

The house was not luxurious nor was it totally finished, yet Tina was pleased. On the main floor, the walls were up and finished, with the bedroom and living room whitewashed, the kitchen and dining area painted with the newfangled washable oil paint. *How nice was that?* The kitchen didn't have cupboards built in; there was a stand-up china cupboard, a wash-stand for dishes, and another small one for hand-washing, a little work table, and, of course, the central wood stove. It was enough.

The bathroom held a cash-and-carry toilet, nothing else. Unless you counted the set of shelves on the east wall. But that, too, was enough.

The fine furniture that they had accumulated – Tina's newly built dresser, Jacob's lovely desk, the new dining room table - all helped to lift the luxury level of the home, as did the hardwood floors. Jacob had gone out of his way to buy a set of several brand new kitchen chairs, the kind with the round back and spindles, as well as a brand new, extra bright kerosene lamp, the type with 2 mantels that hung from a hook in the ceiling in the centre of the dining room.

The children's beds, too, had been built and placed, the baby carriage ready and waiting.

And that's how it had been when Alvin was born, a few days early, on July the 21st.

Again, there were no complications. He, too, was born at home with only the midwife present. He reminded Tina of her brother Bernhard, and she liked that, brawny looking, dark-haired and all. In light of the other things happening before that, it seemed only a drop in the bucket, even though having four children before the oldest was quite three did feel like a big sized challenge.

*   *   *

And that's pretty much how it was, still, a year and a half later, on February the 8th, when Frieda was born. This time, they went to the hospital though. She looked more like the twins did, with large blue eyes, a thick mop of blondish hair that curled just a wee bit, and pretty soon, an impish smile that caused people to call her cute and adorable.

Jacob bonded well with her right from the start. After a day's hard work, he liked nothing better that to bounce her on his swinging foot when he sat on his favourite chair and joyfully make her laugh.

114

Chapter Three

—⟨✺⟩—

The Forties

*W*hile Tina was busy with the babies (who were begin-ning to grow up quickly) and planting huge gardens and helping out with the newly developed farm chores and Jacob was establishing himself as a farmer and finding it not even that bad, there were changes happening and issues brewing in their church community and some of the neighbouring ones as well that pulled *hard* at their heartstrings.

The original concerns behind these things were basically good, Godly even, but the vibes they created could become downrightly unsettling and sometimes worse. One of these concerns began with Jacob's brother Peter and some of his friends. They developed a real passion to bring positive changes into the church. Some worked. Some boomeranged.

One very successful venture was the start of a Sunday school program. Although some were against it, the movement got momentum and soon worked very well. Jacob, while still known as a conservative string-puller, agreed heartily with this one. He remembered his own search for truth in his childhood, and he wanted better for his family. From day one, his children were there every Sunday. And the four classes, (later five) held on the balcony of the old Blumenort Church (located 1 mile south of the present church, where there is a grave yard still), were wonderful.

One trouble spot was Peter's desire to bring more contem-porary singing into the church. Nothing worldly or flashy, just good old gospel songs. The black Gesangbuch that had been used successfully for several generations now had good lyrics but no notes and no choruses. The long verses– most songs had from ten to twenty verses - seemed very dry and boring to the younger generation. And Peter loved every one of his eleven children; he wanted to keep them on board, walking with God, and yes, even loving the church. So, he fought for change; he wanted the church to buy the Evangeliums Lieder*, which should be a good compromise, he thought, still German, still having some of the old songs, but with notes and many more contemporary gospel hymns.

The debate got hot; people were divided, swinging back and forth. One day, Peter's measure was full. He and a friend decided to go buy the books themselves and put them into the church pews. "Luckily," said one of the members who was against it, "I got to church early that Sunday and found them. Quickly, we removed every one. This evil must not be amongst us."

It took several more years for the church to settle that issue. Jacob was not impressed with his brother at the time and carefully let him know. He was not a fighter though, and he was not really against the songs. He actually learned to love several of them greatly, but he hated the hassling, and therefore, voted a firm *no*. Church traditions needed to be respected. Later, it was his baby brother Frank who persuaded him, gently yet passionately, to change his mind.

After a while, it became a non-issue. He and Tina kept that old book at their bedside and used it as their devotional, frequently singing a long song at bedtime, Jacob in his low monotones and Tina in her clear ringing voice – which, to the young children's ears, sounded harmonious and created cherished memories.

There were several other burning issues on the minds of the people. One involved opportunities to keep farming. The general consensus was that Christian families belonged on the farm - not exactly all, but certainly most. The problem was that they were running out of land; everything in the area was taken up. With their large families, this posed a threat to their lifestyle. More and more people were talking about looking elsewhere – maybe it was time to make some major moves.

At about the same time, there was a growing concern among many of the people; they saw worldliness creeping into the church, and it scared them. Some of this came from the Russian Mennonite influence. Those families had gorgeous modern weddings – some even with dancing and suchlike parties, their women's clothing and hairdos were more fashionable and simply too pretty, even the young men were allowed to wear shorts. Shucks! Others had to do with getting a higher education – a very scary thing in itself. Still others with affluence. People could afford fancier cars and things, *but did that make it right?*

For many, *all* of these concerns had a snowball effect, tangled together into one. They needed to find a way out.

* * *

In the summer of 1944, Peter and Maria moved their large family to Carberry. They were in search of land to offer farming opportunities to their children, and they were in search of more freedom to worship according to their heart's desire and to witness of Jesus freely to neighbours.

To Jacob, who had lived with them for thirteen years, this was a big deal. He did not quite know what to do with it. Yet the very next summer, in 1945, he took his whole family, in the model A, for the outing of their lives. All the way to Carberry, where they spent a night, too. On the way there, they stopped at the Assiniboine Park in Winnipeg to see the animals. This was the first and perhaps only time it ever happened. And Betty had the royal adventure of getting lost in the surrounding bush there.

Peter, in hindsight, after the initial settling in was done, struggled some, second guessing himself. They had, after all, located to a strange community that was basically English (no German spoken there); there was no proper home church until they helped create one themselves, many of their neighbours were either non-Christian or were not churchgoers. Yes, they had an attractive large home and lots of land for farming, hilly fields, too, to make it fun, but the deep roots of their upbringing didn't die from the moving. By the time all would be said and done, what would happen to his precious family?

In spite of his trepidation, they stayed, they built up the family home and farm site (where one of his sons still lives happily today), and things turned out well, for the most part, with his family.

*   *   *

More of Jacob's large family got into the moving away mode. Brother David and his wife Helen and stepbrother Frank Klassen and his wife and their lovely children moved to St. Catharines, Ontario, where the abundant fruit gardens grow. They did not feel the need to stick with the farming-is-best theory or the traditional old ways for that matter, so they settled quite happily in their newly chosen home city. There they also found a good church to be involved with, and things went quite well for them.

*   *   *

In Blumenort, the topic of moving out to find more farmland remained a hot one. It surfaced again and again. In the course of time, this would lead them to settle in areas like Riverton, Arborg, Kola, and Wawanesa. Every time the subject came up at a brotherhood meeting (which was a regular event in their church), someone would be sure to inject, "But let's not do it like the Peter Wiebes did. Alone among strangers. That way we would be sure to lose ourselves to the world. So, we must remember to always move in groups, good, solid groups." Jacob agreed with the sentiments but hated the negative connotations. He loved his brother, no matter what.

Before any of these minor migrations took place, a much bigger one happened - one that tore Tina's heart in two and caused them both a major upheaval. But before we go into that, let's jump back a bit to visit Jacob's sister Anna.

Anna, like Jacob, had not married young. She, too, had suffered some early disappointments, she had spent considerable time helping out in various homes among the family, but after a while, she needed more. If only she could have a home of her own! If marriage was not on the horizon for her, shouldn't there be a different way to achieve that?

Jacob got on her bandwagon. Empathy makes a heart go tender. Together with his siblings, he built her a house of her own, a tiny little one, right off the long driveway of the Peter Wiebe place (which Frank bought when the Peter Wiebes moved) at the southwest corner of the Blumenort community. They finished the house nicely, and she loved her new home – except for the bouts of loneliness that struck occasionally.

Jacob loved that place. It stirred up something that he couldn't explain; it put a sparkle into his eyes that was unaccounted for. *Is that something that precious childhood memories can do?* Regardless of all the reasons, he made very sure that, every so often, as the need would arise, like when Tina was sick or perhaps having a baby, he would take one of his children there for a few days. Betty remembers this well, candy jar and all. He would treat this as if it were an honour and privilege – which no doubt it was, and a very important one, too.

On January 1st in 1946, Anna married widower Peter Barkman who had been left very tragically, during his wife's last child birthing, with nine children.

Peter and Anna Barkman would later become part of the core group that migrated to Riverton. Together, they had two lovely daughters.

* * *

1948 was the year of Tina's last baby's birth. On February 14th, Valentine's Day, Jim (Jacob Jr.) was born. He was loved well - perhaps because he was now the only little one around, or perhaps because they'd had so much trouble hanging on to their last babies (they had buried a stillborn three years before and had numerous miscarriages both before and after that) or maybe simply because he was who he was – cute, smart, and good.

But the positive vibes of this praise-the-Lord event could not very well overshadow the other thing that was happening.

1948 was also the year of the unprecedented migration to Mexico - the one that involved numerous families from Blumenort, Kleefeld, Steinbach, Morris, and wherever. *Dozens* of families were involved. The movement was so strong, the arguments so persuasive, that it felt for a while, at least to Jacob and Tina, that everybody who was somebody was going. And anybody who wasn't was the black sheep.

Since Jacob had always been known for his conservative stand, and since being conservative and trying to run away from the worldliness around them was a core issue with this group (among other things, like wanting more land, and less education), everyone expected Jacob to sign up. He did. He bought 100 acres of land in Mexico. Everyone expected him and Tina and family to move with the group; if perhaps, they couldn't quite make it with the main group, they could always join the stragglers who were coming a year or two later.

It became a tug-of-war issue that was not easily resolved.

The fact that *seven* of Tina's siblings decided to join this group, some of them becoming ardent leaders in it, totally complicated things for Tina. How could this have happened? Ma did not raise her family to be super conservative, nor did their home church in Kleefeld. *Where did this all come from?* Tina thought of how her preacher/counsellor had taught her to trust God above all else and how it was not by works and how she had gotten the joy of her salvation that day so long ago now, and though it had sometimes wavered, she refused to let it go – it was too precious.

But now, what if they were right and she was wrong? One of her brothers had told her that they could not expect to see their children safely in heaven some day unless they moved. Here, in this wicked country, they would all be lost. Was that true? If it was, where did that leave her own precious children? Jacob had said they would take their time to make that final decision – so far, they simply didn't know.

When Bernhard had explained his reasons for joining, he was not rough about it; he remained true to himself, gentle and kind. Tina thought her heart would break. Bernhard, her beloved brother who had been so close to her for so long, would move thousands of miles away and perhaps never be seen again? How could she bear that?

And sister Lies, too; now that they both lived in Blumenort, they had gotten so close, always talking on the telephone, often taking their families in their Model A's to visit each other's homes. How could she deal with losing all that?

But this was the physical aspect of it. It was nothing compared to the fear that followed her after Jacob put down his foot and said they were *not* moving. He agreed with a lot of the group's concerns, but some, he said, were pushing too far. He was, after all, on the school board in Blumenort now and not only an ardent fan of the school system, but a devoted enthusiast about making their school one of the best and most Christian ever. Yes, of course, they were a public school, they had to teach English and obey some basic rules, but they had all the liberty in the world as far as he was concerned. They hired only Christian teachers and promoted a strong Christian environment where they taught Bible, Catechism, German, and more. To denounce all that as wrong was more than he could do.

In her heart, Tina agreed with him. It was hard. She was between a rock and a hard place. Especially when, after Jacob's announcement, both of them got a lot of frowning disapproval, bits of harsh criticism, and numerous very solemn warnings.

The angst all this created kept simmering at the bottom of her heart for the rest of her life. Sometimes, it could be lying dormant and almost forgotten but then suddenly flared back to life by some thoughtless remark made by a well-intentioned visitor. It would haunt her, for brief moments at least, even to her final deathbed.

*   *   *

1948.

And suddenly, they were all gone. Some by train, some by car, but gone nonetheless.

Life went on; it had to. There were five school children now – yes, Frieda started school that year, plus Tina had a baby to take care of. There was little time to mope or even grieve her losses unless you counted the times when she thought no one was looking. *No one was supposed to know that.*

It was Christmas, and in this now cruelly made-so-very-lonely season, it surprised Tina that the school's Christmas program which was performed most enthusiastically at the Blumenort Church became a highlight for her. The trustees' families had been asked to sit in the front pew, and she liked that feeling, happily taking 10 month old Jimmy with her. He was a good baby, but he couldn't sit still, so she let him lie on the floor where he gleefully kicked his feet around and played at the pew end with his pudgy little fingers. He may have been a distraction for some of the school boys who tried so hard to make a perfect job of their Vensche* and were almost forced to gawk at him instead. But for her, it was one of the best days of that year. After all the trauma – a real happy hour and a God- send. Her children were what she had left, and they created joy for her.

* * *

A year or two later, another amazing thing happened.

Tina simply couldn't believe it.

Jacob knew how she had struggled because of her bad eye. He had bought her glasses early on, but while that had helped her eyesight, it hadn't corrected the underlying problem. Tina had gotten used to the situation; yet occasional snide remarks had followed her ever since it first happened. *No one ever totally gets used to those.* And Jacob had seen the hurt.

Now, he had heard something that he had to investigate. Bravely, he went to the doctor's office to find out – *was it true?*

It was, and he was elated. There was now a surgery available that could fix bad eyes like Tina's. They could actually go in there, behind the eyeball, and adjust, tighten, and repair the muscles that had been the culprit in the first place. And to answer his further questions, yes, it was safe and worked reliably well.

He came home to share the good news, surprising her royally. The arrangements were made quite quickly and almost before anyone knew what was happening, Tina came home from the hospital with two good *straight* eyes. She was forever grateful.

And yes, Jacob had paid for that out of his own pocket. *Isn't that what a man does when he loves his wife?*

Of course, all surgeries at that time were privately funded.

*   *   *

During the course of the first twelve or so years on the farm, the house slowly but surely got finished. The upstairs held four new bedrooms, not large but each had a closet, was painted nicely, and finished with flooring and doors. Jacob did most of the work, but the family always helped. They also repainted all the rooms downstairs with *good* paint (even though it was more expensive), and the exterior, too.

Creating a modern kitchen was perhaps the biggest assignment in that process, but he made a fine job even though it took a while. Then, when Tina needed to go in for gallstone surgery in 1952, she asked for an electric range. Not for herself, she could live without it, but the doctor had told her she would not be able to do anything for six weeks. The children would be doing the cooking, and it would be so much less hassle that way.

Jacob obliged, and everyone was pleased. And somehow, that old wood stove was never ever seen again. *Where did it stay? Does anyone know?*

Other good things were happening, too. One day, when Tina was again struggling with health issues, Jacob came to her and said he would take over the baking of the bread and buns, especially the kneading of the dough, which was the most strenuous part. He didn't know how, but he would learn.

And learn he did.

The sight of him kneading the dough, in that *big,* round, shiny aluminum bowl, became a standard thing, especially for the youngest two children. And it went on as long as Jacob and Tina lived.

Chapter Four

———◦◦◦———

$\mathscr{J}$acob's sister Tina, who'd been married to Cornelius Reimer since 1928, died tragically in 1940, just 3 months after giving birth to Susie (later Lavina Unger) and left behind six devastated children. Cornelius tried to manage on his own, but it was too much for him. Eventually, the youngest two children, Peter and Susie, were adopted by others, and the other four, together with their father, tried to cope as best they could.

The family lived just down the road, north of Jacob and Tina's house. Jacob was also a Goutmann*, appointed by the church to help out, so he had double reason to get involved. Those children were heavy on Jacob and Tina's hearts all the time; they went through some very rough times. Mary spent the most time at Jacob and Tina's; sometimes, the girls would come running for help at the strangest hours, but they were always welcome.

In 1945, Cornelius married Elizabeth Schroeder, a widow with three children; life slowly started improving for the family, even though the adjustments were neither quick nor easy. In the end, they decided to move to Mexico with the migration group, and the couple had six more children from that relationship. By the sound of things – as Jacob and Tina heard it - they did quite well, too.

*   *   *

Jacob was a community man, never flamboyant but very committed. Besides being a school trustee for years, he was also a telephone man. That meant he was on the board long before MTS time. He was involved with the decision making regarding the placement of new lines, the hiring of an operator for the office, purchasing a supply of telephones, repair parts,

124

and much more. It also meant that although he was not the regular fulltime fix-it man, he was always on call, ready to help out. He understood the system well and thrived on the responsibility.

The school trustee position he took very personally and saw it as his God appointed opportunity to have a positive and helpful influence. When there were struggles, he fought them like a spiritual struggle – deep, intense, determined. When there were victories, he rejoiced in them wholeheartedly, and not once, although there was never any financial retribution, did anyone ever hear him even as much as hint that the efforts and sacrifices required were too much.

*   *   *

Farming had not come easy for Jacob, but he was determined to make a go of it, and he did. Luckily, between the land that he'd inherited from his father and the money he had managed to save when he worked, they were able to operate most of the time without any debt. This was important to Jacob because of the disillusioning twist his well-to-do father had encountered toward the end, and Jacob had determined never to fall into that trap. He'd rather have less and have it paid for than more and lose it in the end.

His sons, as they started growing up, didn't always like this. They wanted more faster. He made some compromises. When he bought the milk quota (a new legal requirement for those who wanted to produce milk and get a guaranteed good price for it), small as it was, he borrowed some money. But with the steady income and being frugal and all, he soon had it all paid up.

Tina helped in the barn, often doing the milking or at least some of it. Once the children were old enough, they took part, too, by hand, of course. It was considered a family affair.

Jacob was never a big horse lover like his father had been, yet he handled his horses well. Taking part in the harvest was his favourite part of farming, and this often consisted of neighbours working together and helping each other out. Toward this end, he would gladly hitch up his team and help a neighbour bring in his green feed or hay perhaps. (Some of those neighbour boys who rode with him on the hayrack when he helped them still have cherished memories about that.) Such things made life worthwhile, and he came home smiling even though he was soaked with sweat and dirt. When it was threshing time, he preferred running the big machine for his brother who owned it, but when he wasn't needed there, he'd also bring in the loads of sheaves with his team of horses. In that sense, he was a bit of a jack of all trades.

Tina loved the threshing bees when it was their turn to host. She'd get up early in the morning to cook up a storm; she'd outdo herself, making the best meal, including a whole array of yummy pies. Everyone in the crew was pleased to be included at her long table and thanked her profusely. Her children got into it, too, and didn't mind the extra work and the countless running of errands.

*   *   *

Their connection with the family members that had moved to Mexico was not as lost as Tina had feared. At first, their only communication was an occasional letter that came. Mexican mail was very unreliable and slow at best. But when a letter did come, it was shared around and rejoiced about.

Then, Jacob surprised her by saying they would go down for a visit. That was heady stuff – travelling by car to Mexico. It wasn't the Model A anymore, but it was a big adventure. It was 1952. Jimmy was 4 ½ and got to go along. The other children were old enough to stay at home. One most unusual exception was made – someone got asked to take a picture of the family so they could take it along to show the relatives. .

Jacob and Tina were gone for about a month, having stopped in Kansas on the way back to revisit the homes she and Bernhard had gone to, now so long ago.

Tina was more than blessed, thankful to the fullest degree. She had seen all the missing members of her family, and for the greater part, they seemed alright. Sure, their start up years had been tough, but that could be expected, couldn't it? Everyone had been happy to see her. No one had found a lot of fault with them, maybe because they, too, had been missed. Jacob even managed to sell his 100 acre piece of land.

When they got home, Jimmy's sisters got the hugs of *their* lifetimes from him. They had been missed! And Jacob determined that this trip was so special and so worthwhile that he wanted to give that to each of his children. He told them that, and he kept his promise. Each of them got a trip to Mexico given to them, arranged by their father, before they reached the age of 21.

*   *   *

Soon, there was another connecting thing. The nieces and nephews who had known and loved Tina through the past years were all grown up now in Mexico. They were getting married and started raising their own families. But they remembered Canada, and many of them got a bit of a restless itch, and they remembered Aunt Tina. One after the other, they came back, some just to visit, some to see a doctor, some actually moved back. But they had no money – only needs, it seemed. And a new crop of little children.

And just like she used to take care of them so many moons ago, Tina took them in. She prepared guest rooms and made up beds. She cooked meals and babysat. She washed and ironed and mended clothing, and she did it all out of love. When there is a big family on your heart, there is room for a lot of loving.

Most of them were appreciative, and a host of new friendships sprung up as a result. Jacob, too, went out of his way in the making of, for him, new friends.

*   *   *

As time went on and more and more of the old ways got deserted to make room for the new, Jacob sometimes felt lost. Combines replaced the threshing machine. Milking machines in the dairy. Younger men trying to take over the boards and committees.

He liked some of that. Operating a combine was fun. He enjoyed those first tractors, too, and loved to watch his sons express their enthusiasm about them. He built a front end loaded hay sweep for a tractor one summer, and somebody told him he'd gone terribly modern.

But some of it threatened him. It felt like handwriting on the wall. *Could he survive all the changes?*

If this trend continued, *would there still be a reason to get up in the morning?*

* * *

One day, Tina, being in a reflective mood and thinking she was alone in the house, spoke aloud to herself. "God has been so good to me, and I will keep trusting Him and serving Him, regardless, no matter what happens." Suddenly, she remembered her song book of old. She went to look for it in the top drawer of her personal dresser. There it was, and it opened naturally to the correct page. Before she could stop herself, she was singing heartily.

Keep on the sunny side.
Always on the sunny side
Keep on the sunny side of life.
It will help you every day
It will guide you all the way.
If only you will keep on the sunny side of life.

She was smiling. She understood that song better today than she ever had.

Suddenly, she heard someone; she gasped as she turned around. *Her daughter had witnessed the whole thing! Really?*

"Don't tell your father," she whispered quickly without thinking. Then, seeming to reconsider, she added, "Ach, maybe it would be okay, he is changing so much . . . . ."

"Does he not like that song?"

"He didn't use to. He said it was too modern, too lively. So, I'd always sing it only when no one was around."

"Well, the other day when we had the singing here, he himself suggested a modern song, didn't he?'

"Yes, indeed. Indeed."

* * *

Jacob *was* mellowing. It may have been part of the aging process, but more likely it had a lot to do with other influences, too. Revival meetings had become the new focus, whole long series of them, and that became *big*, both in their church and many others. The Brunk tent meetings near Steinbach were part of this movement. And Jacob and Tina were ready to go with it.

They and their children attended many, if not most, of the services.

Jacob came home from a service one time with a new conviction, and he started family devotions - one day a week on Sunday mornings. The children were restless and needed time to adjust. Sitting through a whole chapter of bible reading in German monotones seemed long; the girls had had plans to do their hair extra pretty for church. But they learned and eventually appreciated it.

* * *

Tina had just come home from the hospital where she'd visited a dying brother. At the moment, she and Betty were alone in the room. She was obviously troubled.

Suddenly, she blurted it all out. "And they all thought he was out of his mind - didn't know what he was saying. I knew right away. Knew exactly what he meant when he looked at me and said, 'What happened in the barn . . . it was wrong . . . .forgive us . . . forgive us,' and he choked up a bit as I nodded to him. And then he slipped away into unconsciousness again. . . He wasn't the only one involved . . . but I never thought I would hear those words."

The next day when he died, she cried. Then, through the tears, she whispered, "In heaven, all things will be right."

* * *

The family was in crisis mode. One of their sons was going through a very difficult phase, and nobody could do anything to make it better.

Jacob and Tina tried everything they could think of: praying, crying, pleading, arguing, and even asking others for help. Nothing had worked. And the helplessness drove Jacob to his knees like nothing had ever done before.

During one of his most desperate prayer sessions, alone in his room, he saw a vision and heard a voice. "Everything will turn out in the end. Your son will be fine," he was told.

Nothing changed overnight, but Jacob counted those words as a promise, and he clung to them to the end. He had a new spring in his step, too, a sparkle in his eyes again.

This was the beginning of a total shift in his thinking, spiritually speaking. He'd always had a solid faith in God, believing in Jesus for salvation; still, there had remained a missing link. He'd been so busy striving for perfection and evaluating things based on works, he failed to see the need for grace. Not entirely, of course, but to a large extent.

Now, slowly but surely, that had changed.

A number of times, with tears streaming down his face, he gave testimony of this. And he'd always quote a portion of the song that became his new favourite.

Christi Blut und Gerechtigkeit
Das ist mein Schmuck und Ehrenkleid,
Damit werd ich vor Gott bestehen
Wenn Ich zum Himmel werd eingehn.

Loosely translated, that means: Jesus' blood and *His* righteousness is the only honour I can claim; with that, I will stand before God when I get to go to heaven.

* * *

When Jacob and Tina's first grandchild, Jolyn, was born, they were excited and went to visit as soon as possible. While Jacob carefully held and admired the new baby, he suddenly broke down and wept. After he composed himself somewhat, but still in tears, he gazed upward (as if searching for heavenly affirmation perhaps) and said, "Oh, if only . . . if only I could show my Papi. Then he would know, finally, that something good did come out of me, too." The heart-wrenching passion that came with those words proved only one thing – they spoke of his life-long, and still largely unresolved struggle to prove himself to his father, something he'd often concluded was out of his reach.

*   *   *

Life has a way of moving forward through all the many stages. Sometimes, it is a circle, and sometimes, it goes in circles, round and round. But whatever it is or is not, life is always a journey. And the telling of a person's story is always the description of a dash – the dash on your gravestone between your first day and your last.

Glossary

—⁊⁊⁊—

Schoenschreiben - handwriting skills

Plumi Moose – sweetened fruit soup with prunes and raisins in it

Schnetki – old fashioned tea biscuits

Gesangbuch – song book (the thick old style without notes)

Groszer Gott Wir Loben Dich – Great God we praise You

Filafnis - a pre-wedding get-together to honour the couple

Diestel – the center pole at the front of a wagon or sleigh to which horses get hitched

Vensche – Christmas poems

Goutmann – literally a good man; actually, a care-giver appointed by the church to help the needy

Kabitt Schlayde – a sturdy, canvas covered, enclosed sleigh

PlattiHoff – literally Plett Yard; actually, a very small village with mostly Pletts living in it

Papi – Daddy or Dad

Reische Tvieback - toasted buns (done to prevent spoilage)

Evangeliums Lieder – Evangelical Songs, a comparatively modern German songbook with notes and choruses

Epilogue

———✵✵✵———

*S*ome things are worth repeating. Like *hindsight = 20/20 vision.* Or *it's all a matter of perspective.*

Perspective is an intriguing thing; about as reliable as a fleeting shadow, and yet so often, we nail it down as truth. It usually does involve truth, but only as it's seen from one side – my side, of course. Isn't that sad?

When I was hurt by my parents (and my church) as a teen, it was all from my perspective.

My sob-story was true, but I totally missed the other side of it. My parents were probably going through major menopause, both at the same time, and struggling with a host of other issues I knew nothing about; right at the exact same time, I arrived to take on my new fulltime kitchen duties and was there to witness it. I was at home from school against my will, and they were coping with teenagers without their typical level of expertise. Clashes were inevitable. And their marriage was stressed to the max. In hindsight, I don't blame them at all.

Their commitment to each other was in place though, and they survived their crises. Isn't that more than we can say for a lot of people these days?

We all survived and, eventually, flourished. Even my brother, who created such a crisis when he was young, turned out alright, just like father's *voice* of promise had told him, and he died at peace with God and man. Even I, the secret rebel, turned out sort of okay, don't you think?

Going back to their story - if this were a more perfect world, I would have found better pictures, or more, or included vignettes about all the precious relatives, not just some - I might have included other equally important incidents before I ran out of space. If such things seem unfair to you, I apologize.

Also, I need to repeat that the first two chapters of Jacob's story contain a higher dose of creativity than the rest of the book. They're still based on solid facts; I had all the statistics and a lot of clear dots of information, but not enough story to connect them. *So, why didn't I just leave that part alone?* Well, I *needed* that part to figure out who my father was, so I invented a few scenarios and even Great Aunt Margreta to help me with that process. As a result, the story behind the story is factual; details may not be. Does that make sense?

I have my own list of facts and reasons behind every scene. From *my* present perspective, it is the truest and most accurate way of telling a one hundred year old story that's never been documented. And I truly believe that my parents, if they were here to read it, would be both humbled by it and pleased.

If you have questions about that, or any other comments to share, you can reach me at 204-434-6460 or lbbarkman@ xplornet.com. I love to hear from my readers.

Betty Barkman

CPSIA information can be obtained at www.ICGtesting.com
Printed in the USA
LVOW100703301212

313676LV00001B/1/P